THE PARABLES THEN AND NOW

Also by A. M. Hunter

According to John
Design for Life
The Gospel According to St Paul
Gospel and Apostle
The Gospel Then and Now
Interpreting the Parables
Introducing the New Testament
Introducing New Testament Theology
Jesus – Lord and Saviour
Saint Mark
The Epistle to the Romans
The Work and Words of Jesus

The Parables
Then and Now

A. M. HUNTER

SCM PRESS LTD

334 01213 9 $ 33.60

First published 1971
by SCM Press Ltd
58 Bloomsbury Street, London WC1
Fourth impression 1979

Printed in Great Britain by
Fletcher & Son Ltd, Norwich

CONTENTS

PART ONE

1 The Parables of Jesus 9

2 The Story of their Interpretation 16

3 Expounding the Parables Today 23

PART TWO
The Parables Today

4 The Coming and Growth of the Kingdom 35

5 The Grace of the Kingdom 52

6 The Men of the Kingdom 74

7 The Crisis of the Kingdom 89

8 Eternal Issues 108

Select Bibliography 122

Indexes 123

PREFACE

This book is a sequel to my *Interpreting the Parables*, in which the accent fell on the 'Then'. In this one the stress is on the 'Now'; and it seeks to make the parables speak to our predicament today, and that in an existential rather than a merely moralizing way.

My gratitude is due to Miss Kathleen Downham of the SCM Press who prepared the MS for publication and made the indexes; to my Aberdeen neighbour, the Rev. James S. Wood who read the typescript; and to my university colleague, Dr Howard Marshall who read the proofs.

May 1971   A. M. Hunter

PART ONE

I

The Parables of Jesus

The first three gospels contain between fifty and sixty stories, some short, some long, which we call parables. How do you conceive of them?

When I was in my early twenties, I used to think of them as picturesque stories with morals attached, eminently suitable for teaching children in Sunday school. Forty years later, many of these same parables seem to me more like Churchill's speeches in 1940 – weapons of war in a great campaign against the powers of darkness which took Jesus to the cross. This is the measure of the revolution in our understanding of them which we owe to modern scholars. There have been two chief factors in it. One has been the rediscovery of the true meaning of the kingdom of God which is the main burden of the parables. We now realize that the phrase should be interpreted eschatologically and dynamically, that it means the sovereign rule of God decisively invading history in the ministry of Jesus, and that the parables, which form a kind of running commentary on it, are instruments of controversy in the fulfilment of a transcendent purpose which reached a climax at Calvary. The other factor has been the application of 'Form Criticism' to the gospels. By a wise use of this new gospel science we have been largely able to lay bare the original form of the parables before the church used them for its own purposes, and so to recover the original thrust of the parables as Jesus spoke them. The result is that we may now claim to understand them better than any Christians since the apostolic age.

But this is to anticipate conclusions: we had better begin at the beginning.

In Sunday school we learned to define a parable as 'an earthly story with a heavenly meaning'. This is true enough, so far as it goes. Rather different is the definition of a parable given by one of P. G. Wodehouse's characters. A parable, he says, is one of those stories in the bible which sounds at first like a pleasant yarn, but keeps something up its sleeve which suddenly pops up and knocks you flat. True, again. Some parables contain 'the ambush of the unexpected'. Nathan's parable of the Little Ewe Lamb (II Sam. 12.1-14) is one such. To the same category belong Christ's parables of the Two Debtors (Luke 7.40-43), the Good Samaritan (Luke 10.25-37) and the Wicked Vinedressers (Mark 12.1-12).

However, to please the pundits, we had better be a little more precise. The word 'parable', Greek in origin, means a 'comparison'. We may then define a parable as a comparison drawn from nature or from daily life, and designed to teach some spiritual truth, on the assumption that what is valid in one sphere – nature or daily life – is also valid in the spiritual world. And this means in the gospels the kingdom of God – God's saving sovereignty in action and the new order of things thus established – which is the burden of Jesus' 'good news' or gospel.

The next point is that parable is a form of *teaching* – often, if you like, polemical teaching. Dean Inge has said, 'Almost all teaching consists in comparing the unknown with the known, the strange with the familiar'. It is a matter of everyday experience that you cannot explain anything except by saying that it is *like* something else, something more familiar. So the gospel parable often begins, 'The kingdom of God is like . . . – like leaven, or like a mustard seed, or like a drag net'. What Jesus means is, 'If you want to understand how God rules . . .' or, 'Here is how things work out under the rule of God . . .' Only notice that you cannot stop at 'The kingdom of God is like . . .' You must follow the story through to the end. The kingdom of God is not like leaven but like what happens when you put leaven into a batch of flour – a heaving, panting mass, all motion, bubbles and explosive energy.

Combine, then, this method of teaching by analogy with the Oriental's liking for pictorial speech and Everyman's love of a good story, and you have most of the reasons why men took to using parable, to convey truth in a challenging way.

Parables, of course, are found in the Old Testament as well as in the New, as we also find them in the teaching of the rabbis. Notice, too, that the Hebrew word for parable, *mashal*, is a wide label for all kinds of figurative speech – from a simple metaphor to an elaborate story. So it is with the gospel parable. 'Physician, heal yourself', is a parable (Luke 4.23), though it has only three words; but so also is the Prodigal Son, which has nearly four hundred.

At its simplest, therefore, a parable is a figurative saying, sometimes a simile like, 'Be you wise as serpents', sometimes a metaphor like, 'Beware of the leaven of the Pharisees'. What we are accustomed to call parables are simply expansions of these. 'All we like sheep have gone astray', is a simile. Expand it into a *picture*, and you get what is called a 'similitude', e.g. the parable of the Lost Sheep. Expand it into a *story* by using past tenses, and you get a story-parable like the Great Supper.

The gospel parables are mostly either similitudes or story-parables.[1] The difference is this. The similitude describes some common everyday process – like putting a patch on a coat or yeast into flour, whereas the story-parable describes not what men commonly do but what one man did: 'A sower went out to sow'; 'A man made a great supper'.

What then is the difference between parables and allegories? Although one or two of Jesus' parables come close to being allegories, and others have allegorical traits, most of them are not. The chief difference to grasp is that whereas in an allegory, like the *Pilgrim's Progress*, each detail in the story has its counterpart in the meaning, by contrast, in the parable, e.g. the Unjust Steward, story and meaning meet not at every point but at one central point (called by scholars the *tertium comparationis*). In the example cited, it is the steward's resourceful resolution in a crisis. In other words, the allegory has to be deciphered point by point like a message in code. In the parable proper there is

---

[1] Three or four are 'example stories', e.g., the Good Samaritan, the Rich Fool, the Pharisee and the Publican. These work rather differently. Whereas the parable proper provides an analogy, arguing that what is admitted in one case can hardly be contested in another, the 'example story' produces an illustration from reality and says, 'Go and do (or not do) likewise.'

one chief point of likeness between the story and its meaning –
the picture part and the reality part – and the details simply
make the story realistic and serve the main thrust of the parable,
like the weathers which wing the arrow to its mark.

With these distinctions made, we may now notice three fea-
tures of our Lord's parables.

First: they follow the rules of popular story-telling. Down the
centuries men have found that stories are told more effectively if
you follow certain rough anecdotal rules. One is 'the rule of contrast', whereby virtue and vice, riches and poverty, wisdom and
folly are sharply contrasted. Gospel examples are: The Wise
and the Foolish Bridesmaids, the Rich Man (Dives) and Lazarus,
and the Two Builders. Another is 'the rule of three', whereby
your story has three characters ('An Englishman, an Irishman
and a Scotsman . . .'). Gospel examples are the three travellers in
the Good Samaritan, the three excuse-makers in the Great Supper,
and the three servants in the Talents. And a third is 'the rule of
end stress', whereby the spotlight falls on the last person or act
in the series – whether it is the youngest son or the final adventure. Think, for example, of the 'barren rascal' in the story of
the Talents, or the sending of the only son in the Wicked Vinedressers.

The second point is that Jesus' parables were extemporized in
living encounter with men rather than slowly elaborated and
'lucubrated' like sermons in ministers' studies. They arise out of
'real life' situations and often reflect the cut-and-thrust of the
'holy war' in which Christ was engaged. Thus the three great
parables of Luke 15 – the Lost Sheep, the Lost Coin and the
Prodigal Son – are all ripostes to scribes and Pharisees who had
criticized Jesus for consorting with publicans and sinners. Again,
other parables – like the Barren Fig Tree, the Defendant, the Ten
Bridesmaids and the Wicked Vinedressers – utter warnings and
sound 'alerts' to the rulers and people not to be caught unawares
by the great crisis overhanging God's chosen race.

The third point follows from this. Every parable was meant
to strike for a verdict or to evoke a response in action. 'What do
you think?', Jesus often begins a parable; and where the actual
words are wanting, they are implied. 'He who has ears to hear,
let him hear,' Jesus often concludes. 'Hear' means 'heed', and

what the sentence says in effect is 'This is more than just a pleasant story. Go and work it out for yourselves, and decide.'

All we have been saying paves the way for the question, Why did Jesus use parables? It is not enough to say, Because Jesus recognized that 'truth embodied in a tale' will 'enter in at lowly doors' where abstract talk will fail. True, they quicken understanding by putting truth in a vivid way, but always they are designed to challenge men to action – to make men '*do* the truth'. The parable says, 'See, judge, act'. Yet we must also recognize that the gospel parable is not always clear as daylight nor is it meant to be.[2] It is meant to make people think – even think furiously – and to issue in decision and action. Seen thus, the parable is not to be confused with the 'illustration' in a modern sermon, which so often serves as sugar-coating for the theological pill. The parable, as T. W. Manson[3] reminds us, is not a crutch for limping intellects, but a spur to spiritual perception; and mostly it challenges to choice and decisive action – is existential.

From the question *why* let us turn now to the question *where*. Where did Jesus get the stuff of his parables?

The short answer is: from the real world all round him, the world of nature and of human nature. As Sir Edwin Arnold said:

> The simplest sights we met:
> The Sower flinging seeds on loam and rock,
> The darnel in the wheat, the mustard tree
> That hath its seed so little, and its boughs
> Wide-spreading; and the wandering sheep; and nets
> Shot in the wimpling waters – drawing forth
> Great fish and small – these and a hundred such
> Seen by us daily, never seen aright,
> Were pictures for him from the book of life,
> Teaching by parable.

Even larger in the parables bulk 'the human situation' and the lives of ordinary men and women in home, or farm, or market, or even law court. The Leaven must go back to the time when Jesus watched 'Mary his mother' hiding the yeast in the meal. The Splinter and the Plank (as also the little parable of the

---

[2] On the difficult verses in Mark 4.10-12, see C. F. D. Moule's discussion in *Neotestamentica et Semitica*, Edinburgh 1969, 95-113.

[3] *The Teaching of Jesus*, Cambridge 1935, 73.

Apprenticed Son in John 5.19f.) must go back to the Nazareth
workshop when:

> The Carpenter of Nazareth
> Made common things for God.

The parable of the Playing Children,

> We piped for you and you would not dance,
> We wept and wailed, and you would not mourn (Matt. 11.17)

takes us back to a Nazareth street where lads and lasses 'made
believe' at weddings or at funerals. (It was the boys who played
at weddings, the girls at funerals.) Then as now there were
labourers who hung about in the market-place because 'no man
had hired them', not to mention bridesmaids who skimped their
preparations for a wedding. Probably the Galilee of Jesus' day
knew a rascally manager who was the original of the Unjust
Steward. And so on.

In all this one thing is clear. Jesus believed that human life
with all its faults and frailties could furnish pointers to the rule
of God, and that our human care and concern could figure forth
the care and concern of the Almighty Father. 'If you then, bad
as you are,' he said in the little story of the Asking Son, 'know
how to give your children what is good for them, how much
more will your heavenly Father give good things to those who
ask him' (Matt. 7.11.)

One final question. Can you be sure that we have the parables
substantially as Jesus told them?

The answer is Yes, and for various reasons. For one thing, in
many parables the background is authentically Palestinian. In
the Sower, for example, sowing *precedes* ploughing, as it still
does in Palestine today. If 'we plough the fields and scatter', they
scatter and then plough the fields. (In parables like the Sower
and the Mustard Seed, Jesus' original Aramaic almost glimmers
through Mark's Greek.[4]) For a second point, the parables reveal
Jesus' highly individual way of thinking and speaking – the daring
faith in God (e.g. in his parables on prayer), the swift surprises of
thought so characteristic of him, the many flashes of hyperbole

---

[4] See M. Black, *An Aramaic Approach to the Gospels and Acts*,[3] Oxford
1954, 63, 165.

and even humour which we know were his. And, for a third and more general consideration, it is worth noting that great parables are evidently so hard to create that it is difficult to name another person in history with more than one or two good ones to his credit.

We may therefore be sure that in the parables we are in direct contact with the mind of Jesus. They represent a part of what Jeremias calls 'the original rock of the tradition'.

Nevertheless, one change the parables did undergo in the thirty or forty years that elapsed between Jesus' speaking of them and the time when they were written down in our gospels. In the time of what is called 'the oral tradition', when as yet there was no New Testament and the Christian message was passed from mouth to mouth, the parables took on a new lease of life as the apostles and early Christian preachers used them in their preaching and teaching; and inevitably they re-employed and re-applied them to their own situation and that of their hearers.[5] Thus the parable of the Lost Sheep which Jesus originally addressed to the Pharisees and scribes and which spoke of the redemptive joy of God at a sinner's repentance, became, in the early preachers' use of it, a summons to pastoral concern for lapsing church members. (See Matt. 18.12ff.) Similarly, they re-applied some parables to their own situation 'between the times' (between Christ's first and second comings). Thus the story of the Ten Bridesmaids which had been on Jesus' lips a rousing 'Be prepared!' to his countrymen, in view of the imminent crisis for Israel created by his ministry, has become, in Matthew's re-application, a call to be ready for Christ's coming in glory.

Some people are disconcerted to learn that the early preachers thus re-audienced and re-applied their Lord's parables to fit their own situation. But why should we fault the early Christians for doing this when similar things are done every Sunday (and rightly) by Christian preachers today? Indeed this is the very enterprise we shall be engaged on in the second part of this book.

---

[5] See J. Jeremias, *The Parables of Jesus*, London 1963, Ch. 2.

2

The Story of their Interpretation

From the apostolic age to the present day Christian scholars have been wrestling with the meaning of the parables. In this chapter we shall deal very briefly with their labours from the second century to the twentieth – say, from Irenaeus, bishop of Lyons, to Joachim Jeremias of Göttingen.

In the early centuries of the Christian church the fathers like Irenaeus, Tertullian, Origen and Augustine treated the parables as allegories. In the allegory (we may recall) each detail of the story is a separate metaphor with a meaning of its own which needs to be discovered. By contrast, the parable proper enforces one main point, and the rest is realistic trimming. Thus the parable of the Prodigal Son proclaims one sovereign truth – the free forgiveness of God for the penitent sinner – while, at the same time, gently rebuking self-righteousness in the shape of the elder brother. But note what happened when the early church father, Tertullian, got busy expounding it. The elder son in the story is the Jew, the younger the Christian. The patrimony of which the younger son claimed his share is that knowledge of God which a man has by his birthright. The citizen in the far country to whom he hired himself is the devil. The robe given to the returning prodigal is that sonship which Adam lost at the Fall. The ring is the sign and seal of baptism; the feast is the Lord's Supper; and who is the fatted calf slain for the feast but Christ himself?

It is all very ingenious, but it is not history – or at any rate natural exegesis. It is interpretation in terms of current dogmatic theology.

This sort of allegorical exegesis was to hold the field for many centuries. You see it going on in the writings of Thomas Aquinas at the far end of the Middle Ages. At the Reformation Martin Luther, who condemned it as 'monkey tricks', did not, in his own practice, keep himself free from it. An honourable exception was John Calvin who had a nose for the natural meaning of a parable and a way of going for its main point. So had a Spanish Jesuit called Maldonatus (1533-83) who found himself accused by the Sorbonne of heresy!

But it was not till the nineteenth century, with the rise of scientific study of the bible, that there came a new approach to the interpretation of the parables and an end to this wholesale allegorizing of them. Students will find an excellent account of this progress in understanding the parables in the first chapter of G. V. Jones' *Art and Truth of the Parables* (1964). Suffice it here to say that in this country A. B. Bruce of Glasgow pioneered the new approach in his *Parabolic Teaching of Christ*. But it was about the last decade of last century, and in Germany, that this centuries-long allegorizing of the parables received its *coup de grâce*. The writer was the German Liberal scholar, Adolf Jülicher, and his book *Die Gleichnisreden Jesu* (Vol. I 1888; Vol. II 1899), which unfortunately was never translated into English.

Jülicher's achievement was to prove, by and large, that the parables are not allegories to be spelt out point by point like the clues in a crossword puzzle. On the contrary, they exist mostly to make one point (though, as in the Prodigal Son, there may be a subsidiary one, viz. the rebuke of the self-righteous Pharisee), and the details are part of the dramatic machinery of the story.

But if the parables as a rule make one point, what kind of point is it? It was here that Jülicher, having rightly insisted on the one point, went on, Irishly enough, to miss it. His capital mistake was to make the parables teach moral commonplaces, or platitudes. Thus, for Jülicher, the meaning of the Talents is, 'A reward is only earned by performance'; and of the Unjust Steward, 'Wise use of the present time is the condition of future happiness'.[1] But was Jesus really this kind of person? Did he go about Galilee pointing 'morals' for the multitudes by means of pleasant or

[1] These remind you of the truisms to be seen on 'The Wayside Pulpit' in our big cities, e.g. 'Friendship is proved in adversity'. Men don't need a Jesus to tell them this!

provocative stories? Jülicher never faced the literally 'crucial' question why a man who went about telling people stories of this kind should have ended up on a gibbet.

His work, however, did prepare the way for the real trailblazer, C. H. Dodd, whose *Parables of the Kingdom*, appearing in 1935, opened up a new era in their interpretation. What then did Dodd do which Jülicher had failed to do? The answer is: he put the parables of Jesus back into their original historical setting which is the ministry of Jesus seen as the decisive, saving activity of God in which the old Israel died and the new Israel was born. The phrase 'realized eschatology' was of Dodd's coining; and if nowadays we agree that 'inaugurated', not 'realized', is the *mot juste*, our debt to the great little Welshman remains undiminished.

When in 1947 Joachim Jeremias of Göttingen produced his classical study *The Parables of Jesus*, he began it by saying that it was unthinkable that there should ever be any retreat from Dodd's basic insights. On Dodd's foundations he built his own book, his own special contribution being a thorough and wise application of the principles of Form Criticism to the parables in order to lay bare their original form and recover their primal thrust on the lips of Jesus.

We have said that Dodd and Jeremias, one after the other, set themselves to restore the parables of Jesus to their true historical setting, which is the ministry of Jesus seen as the sovereign activity of God in which he visited and redeemed his people.

But question: are not the parables already in that setting? The answer is that some are, but some are not. The parable of the Wicked Vinedressers obviously is – it clearly belongs to the closing days of Jesus' ministry in Jerusalem. But what about the Labourers in the Vineyard which, according to Matthew, seems to be addressed to the disciples, and, was Jesus talking to his disciples about the right use of money (as Luke 16.10-13 seems to imply) when he told the story of the Unjust Steward?

At this point we may recall (what was said in chapter 1) that the early preachers took our Lord's parables and sometimes re-applied and re-audienced them to suit the situation of their own hearers. Once this is realized – and Dodd and Jeremias have made the point plain – we can set about restoring any re-applied parables to their original setting in the life and ministry of Jesus. What is it? We must spend a little more time explicating it, if our exegesis of the parables is to be sound and any modern exposition of them erected on a truly critical foundation.

All Jesus' parables have to do, in one way or another, with the coming of the kingdom of God (*basileia tou theou*). This phrase signifies the reign, or sovereignty, of God in action and the new order of things thus established. To understand all it implies, we must remember that for centuries the Jews had been praying for the time when the living God would really take to himself his great power and reign. Now it was the very heart of Jesus' 'good news' that the kingdom of God was dawning (Mark 1.15, 'The time has come; the kingdom of God is upon you'), that this blessed time was no longer a shining hope on the far horizon but an inbreaking reality. The arm of the Lord was being revealed; God was really beginning to rule. And, as we read on in the gospels, we can see that the whole ministry of Jesus – his preaching, teaching and healing – is in fact the inauguration of that kingdom, God acting in his royal power, God vanquishing the forces of evil that hold man in thrall.

This is the true background of Jesus' parables – the great campaign of the kingdom of God, with Jesus as its spearhead, against the kingdom of evil; and once we understand this, we see how the parables fall into their proper historical setting and become pregnant with point and meaning.

We may now arrange the chief parables into four groups each of them illustrating some aspect or phase of the kingdom of God.

1. First, *the Coming and Growth of the Kingdom*

When the Old Testament prophets had pictured God's action in the new age, they had often depicted him as the Great Sower (Hos. 2.23; Jer. 31.27; Ezek. 36.9; Zech. 10.9. Cf. Isa. 55.10f.).

Accordingly, in the gospels five parables tell how the Great Sower's kingdom comes and grows. With certainty and to great and unimaginable endings, say the two parables of the Mustard Seed and the Leaven. Quietly, but nevertheless irresistibly, says the story of the Seed growing Secretly. In spite of all hazards and failures, yielding a fine harvest, says that story of a farmer's fortunes which we call the Sower. But the rich crop can only be fully gathered in through my death, says Jesus in the little similitude about the Grain of Wheat.

But Jesus does not confine himself wholly to images from agriculture. He sees the kingdom of God as a great Supper to which the invitation goes out, 'Come, for all things are now ready,' or (talking to fishermen) he conceives it as a Drag Net which sweeps into its meshes all sorts of fish.

2. The second group of parables may be entitled *the Grace of the Kingdom* because they deal with 'the wideness of God's mercy' to sinners.

'Grace' may be defined as God's extravagant goodness to un-deserving men, and in all the parables of this group – from the little parable of the Two Debtors (Luke) to the much longer tale of the Labourers in the Vineyard (which would be better entitled, as we shall see, the Good Employer) in Matthew – this is the dominant theme. In this latter parable Jesus is saying, 'The rewards of the kingdom are not to be measured by men's deserts but by God's goodness'. This was in answer to the Pharisees who had criticized Jesus for offering the blessings of God's kingdom to tax-collectors and sinners. For the strange thing is that all these parables about the wideness of God's mercy were spoken to his critics in defence of his 'good news'. All three parables in Luke 15 – the Lost Sheep, the Lost Coin and the Waiting Father (commonly called the Prodigal Son) – say in effect, 'If a man will be at such pains to recover his lost property, how much more does God desire to save his lost children! This is what the Almighty is like, and this is why, as his Agent, or Envoy, I am acting as I am.'

3. The third group of parables describes *the Men of the Kingdom*.

To be a disciple of Jesus is to be 'in the kingdom', since where Jesus is, there is the kingdom, i.e. he himself is and embodies the kingdom. The parables in this group all suggest the true meaning of discipleship. Before men decide to follow Jesus, to become 'men of the kingdom', they must sit down and reckon the cost, say the twin parables of the Tower Builder and the Warring King. But to win its riches is worth any sacrifice, say the parables of the Hidden Treasure and the Costly Pearl. In the little tale of the Farmer and his Man Jesus reminds his disciples that they are servants of God and must not try (as the Pharisees did) to claim 'credit' with him. In the stories of the Disobliging Neighbour and the Callous Judge (better known as the Friend at Midnight and the Importunate Widow), Jesus calls for a faith and a prayer which refuse to take No for an answer and ever expect great things from God! And in the parable of the Two Builders (which ends his 'Sermon' in Matt. 7 and Luke 6), he demands a profession that issues in action and tells his men that in the storms of life it will be 'My Way, which is God's Way – or disaster'.

4. Finally, we come to an important group of parables all dealing with *the Crisis of the Kingdom*.

Here we need to remember that Jesus saw his ministry, which was the inauguration of God's kingdom, moving to a great climax or crisis in God's dealings with his people, a crisis which would involve not only the Messiah's death and victory and the rise of a new Israel, but also doom on the Jewish nation and temple. Against this background many of Jesus' parables become luminous with meaning.

In the Barren Figtree and the Defendant on his way to court he bids his countrymen be alive to the gravity of their situation, as in 'the Contemptuous Guests' (alias the Great Supper) he points to the peril of disregarding God's call. In the Savourless Salt and the Talents (Money in Trust) he tells Israel's leaders they will be held accountable before God for their unfaithful stewardship of his revelation. In the Waiting Servants, the Ten Bridesmaids and the Unjust Steward he warns his hearers not to be caught unprepared in the approaching crisis and (like the steward) to act with resolution in it. So Jesus seeks to alert them to the Great Emergency for Israel – God's time of destiny for his chosen people – now at their doors.

But, alas, as he said (Luke 19.41-4), Israel 'did not recognize God's moment when it came' or 'the way that leads to peace' (NEB), and the great drama moved inexorably to its climax.

So the Son of Man, the speaker of the parables, and the chief actor in the drama, marched on Jerusalem where, on an April morning in the year AD 30, the crisis culminated in a crucifixion outside the northern wall of Jerusalem. One parable, that of the Wicked Vinedressers (which we have named 'the Owner's Son') preserves Jesus' final appeal to his nation and its leaders. It is 'Love's last appeal' to a rebellious people. No full-length parable survives to tell how Jesus the Messiah conceived the purpose of his dying – though St John preserves a short one about the Grain of Wheat which must die if it is to bear a rich harvest. Yet three parables in miniature take us some way into the Lord's secret – his three sayings about the Cup, the Baptism and the Ransom. The Messiah is drinking 'the cup our sins had mingled'; he is undergoing a baptism of blood whereby others may be cleansed; as the Servant Messiah he is giving his life to ransom a countless multitude.

What was the sequel? Did the day of reckoning come for old Israel? Did the grain of wheat which fell into the ground and died, bear its rich harvest? Was it given to Jesus the Servant Messiah to 'vindicate many, himself bearing the penalty of their guilt' and to see the Lord's cause prospering in his hand?

The church of Christ is built on the belief that it was. By the resurrection and the gift of the Holy Spirit the kingdom of God came 'with power'. 'When thou hadst overcome the sharpness of death,' says the *Te Deum*, 'thou didst open the kingdom of heaven to all believers.'

3

Expounding the Parables Today

In the previous chapter we sought to summarize 'the new look' that has come over the parables through the work of C. H. Dodd and Joachim Jeremias. But New Testament science never stands still, and in the last two or three decades certain significant trends have been emerging which warrant a further chapter of introduction.

But before we come to them, let us mention two recent discoveries. First, about fifteen parables are to be found in *The Gospel of Thomas*, that farrago of strange sayings of Jesus discovered in the Gnostic Library at Nag Hammadi in 1945. Eleven are variant, and not very veridical, versions of parables in the synoptic gospels. Of the four new ones, two – the Big Fish and the Assassin – may have some slender claim to authenticity; but, all in all, these 'Gnostic' parables add little to our knowledge.

More interesting has been the rediscovery, again due to C. H. Dodd (in his *Historical Tradition in the Fourth Gospel*, 1963), of some ten brief parables in John's gospel which up till then had been supposed innocent of parable. None of them is on the same scale as the great parables in the synoptic gospels; but small 'Johannine' parables like the Apprenticed Son, the True Shepherd, the Benighted Traveller, the Woman in Labour, and the Grain of Wheat, are every bit as authentic as the Hidden Treasure and the Costly Pearl or the Tower Builder and the Warring King, and they add their own little quota of light to the place Jesus knew himself to hold in God's dealings with Israel and, through Israel, with the world.

We come now to the first of the trends already mentioned, viz. the small but spirited revolt against Jülicher's denial of all allegory to Jesus. It is now generally agreed that Jülicher erred when, starting from the Greek concept of parable, he failed to remember that the Hebrew word for it, *mashal*, includes allegory as well as parable, and that he did his work with too much Teutonic vigour and rigour.

The Old Testament, which was Jesus' bible, contains pure allegories, like Ezekiel's of the Eagles and the Vine (Ezek. 17) as well as pure parables like Nathan's about the Little Ewe Lamb (II Sam. 12). Many of the parables the rabbis told were strongly allegorical. It was therefore antecedently likely that Jesus' parables would contain a modicum of allegory. As indeed they do. The Wicked Vinedressers is an allegorical parable. The Sower, which contains three or four different points of comparison, hovers between parable and allegory. (C. F. D. Moule calls it 'a multiple parable'.) The Great Supper contains, in my view and not mine only, allegorical elements. And in others like the Wedding Guests and the Mustard Seed we should not let the shade of Jülicher affright us from admitting allegory. That is to say, 'the bridegroom' (Mark 2.10. Cf. John 3.29) is a veiled reference to the Messiah, and 'the birds of the air' (Luke 13.19) alludes to the Gentiles.

This is not to deny the general truth of Jülicher's thesis, which remains valid and valuable. We are merely saying that he overplayed a good hand. We are asserting that no aesthetic scruple would have prevented Jesus using allegory if and when it suited his purpose, and that if we find in some parables what look very like allegorical traits, we should have the courage to call Jülicher's bluff.

A good working rule would be this. When interpreting, don't try to eliminate everything allegorical – as even Jeremias still tends to do – and so trim them into pure parables. On the other hand, never allegorize to the point which mars the one lesson, or warning, or challenge, which the parable was meant to convey.

The second trend may be called Christological. It is the perception that in some of his parables, if we have ears to hear, we may hear Jesus making veiled claims to Messianic authority or speaking as one who embodies in his own person the destiny of Israel.

We may recall how the early church fathers had a way of

finding Christ *passim* in the parables: Jesus was himself the Good
Samaritan in the tale about 'the Path of Blood', as they called the
road from Jerusalem to Jericho. He was even 'the fatted calf'
slain for the feast in the story of the Prodigal Son. And so on.
Modern scholars rightly abjure such exegetical ingenuities. What
they find in the parables is not explicit but implicit Christology.

Readers who remember the last paragraph of the first English
edition of Jeremias' *Parables of Jesus* (1954) may recall how he
quoted a German scholar, Ernst Fuchs, on the Christological self-
witness of the parables: 'When a parable described God's goodness, it is the goodness which is made effective by Jesus. When
a parable speaks of the Kingdom, then Jesus is hidden behind the
Kingdom as its secret content.' Jeremias warmly agreed with this
thesis, and in the revised English edition of his book (1963), he
has been at pains to bring this point out when it arises.

None of the parables deals directly with Jesus' person – though
the Wicked Vinedressers comes very near to doing so. But
Christological overtones are audible in, say, small parables like
the Stronger Man or the Apprenticed Son (John), in the great
parables of Luke 15, in John's parable of the True Shepherd and
Luke's of the Great Supper, as well as in the Two Builders and
the Last Judgment in Matthew.

But the most convincing statement of this new trend is to be
found not in the work of the German pioneers (like Fuchs) of the
so-called 'New Quest of the Historical Jesus' but in C. W. F.
Smith's *The Jesus of the Parables* which came out in 1948, roughly
a decade before 'the New Quest' got under way. As Smith shows,
in his parables and especially those he uttered on the way to
make his final challenge in Jerusalem, we see Jesus as the central
figure and precipitant of the great crisis which culminated in
the cross and all that followed it, saying things which none
short of the Messiah had the right to say and knowing himself
to be the sole bearer of Israel's destiny, so that at the last, when
he hung on the cross, he was in very truth Israel himself (as he
had claimed to be in the Upper Room when he said, 'I am the
true Vine', John 15.1).

In studying the parables we ought, therefore, to keep our ears
open for this note of sovereign authority; for the parables no less
than the cross pose the problem of Christ's person. They impel

us to ask, Who can this be in whom God's kingdom – his saving sovereignty – is centred, who knows himself to be the all-decisive person in God's ways with Israel and, through Israel, with the wider world?

The last trend to be mentioned is the modern attempt to lift the parables out of their first-century setting where a rather academic criticism has been apt to confine them, and make them speak meaningfully to men today: in short, to expound them existentially.

Years ago I remember the late Ronald Gregor Smith, then Editor of the SCM Press, saying to me, 'If only I could find somebody to do for the modern man what T. W. Manson has done so admirably for the student of the New Testament in his *Sayings of Jesus*.' He might better have instanced the work of Dodd and Jeremias on the parables. For when they have put back the parables into what they think is their original setting, you sometimes wonder if they have not made them so historically time-bound – so locked them away in a first-century Jewish strait-jacket – that Jesus' ripostes in parable to carping Pharisees, his warnings to hot-headed Zealots, and his *ad hominem* challenges to Israel's rulers have little obvious relevance for us today in this so different twentieth century. What Gregor Smith, who was deeply influenced by Rudolf Bultmann, had in mind was an existential approach to Jesus' sayings.

'Existentialism' is the way of thinking we trace back to Kierkegaard (1813-55), that great and gloomy Dane in whom Hamlet was mastered by Christ. It is the philosophy which concerns itself with human experience and tries to understand it out of the concrete experience which, as 'existents', we all have. To think existentially is to think not as a spectator of the ultimate issues of life but as one committed to a decision on them. (It is the sort of thinking a man does when, as a lover, he declares his passion, when as a statesman he commits his country to war, or when as a dying man he clings to his faith.) For the existentialist truth is something to be done. One learns it not from the balcony but on the road: and knowledge of God's truth becomes ours in the act of deciding for it with all that in us is (cf. John 7.17). Born in concern, existential thinking involves response, commitment and obedience.

Now the parables of Jesus almost cry out for such exposition. First, by their very nature, they are not didactic propositions but invitations to decision. Unlike the illustrations in our modern sermons, they are not crutches for limping intellects but spurs to perception – and action. Addressed to a particular historical situation, they aim to win agreement and challenge to decision for or against the kingdom of God. And a successful parable alters the situation and becomes what the Germans call 'a language event'.[1] Second, the very stuff of the parables is human existence – men, women and children, at work or at play, in their hopes and their fears and their anxieties, in their successes and their failures. Third, the subject-matter of the parables – God's will, the nature and growth of his kingdom, the centrality of his mercy, and the response required of his people – are obviously themes which still concern us today, for the simple reason that the church as the new Israel is faced before God with the same responsibilities as the old Israel, as it is ever liable to the judgments which fall on 'the household of faith'.

No question then that it is legitimate to existentialize the parables. Ah but, as 'there is blue and better blue', so there is existentialism and existentialism. Today in Germany former students of Rudolf Bultmann (like Fuchs) are busy producing what they call 'a new hermeneutic' – a new way of interpreting Jesus' words to make them speak to men today. Its two main ingredients are the existentialism of Bultmann's old Marburg colleague, Martin Heidegger, and a revised version of Bultmann's theology. The first, as David Cairns[2] has shown, is a very perilous cradle in which to lay the gospel because, apart from its obscurity, it is doubtfully theistic. The second element is still vitiated by what T. W. Manson called 'the disseminated scepticism' of Bultmann. Add to these the 'splarge' and murkiness of the Fuchs style, and the resultant mixture can hardly be called appetizing. God help the humble hearer in the pew if before he can understand a parable of Jesus he must first be indoctrinated in Heidegger's philosophy of Being and then in Bultmann's theology!

A more helpful approach is that of G. V. Jones in his *Art and Truth of the Parables* (1964). He rightly argues that the great

---

[1] See note at end of this chapter.
[2] *A Gospel without Myth?*, London 1960.

parables of Jesus are works of art ('Perfection beyond compare' was Tennyson's verdict on them), and that any serious work of art has significance beyond its original intention. We are therefore warranted in applying them to situations never contemplated at the time when they were spoken. To show how a parable can escape the captivity of time, he expounds the Prodigal Son in existential terms, so that it becomes an account of man's spiritual predicament today as reflected in contemporary literature and philosophy. The weakness of the book is that it concentrates on the existential at the expense of the evangelical or theological. For we do not fully understand a parable till the question, What does it teach about God? is set alongside the question, What does it teach about man's situation? Man's need is not merely existential, but above all evangelical – 'a Word from the Beyond for our human predicament'. And the answer to that need is not simply self-understanding but that knowledge of God which we owe uniquely to the teller of the parables.

If finally we ask who, in practice, has most effectively existentialized the parables, the answer must be: Helmut Thielicke of Hamburg in his book *The Waiting Father*. Here and there in his exegesis he might have learned from Jeremias; but, take it all in all, this book combines a fidelity to the New Testament with an insight into the contemporary situation and an ability to speak to believers, half-believers and unbelievers which mark out Thielicke as perhaps the greatest scholar-cum-preacher of the day. Two random quotations may hint how existential he can be: 'God is only known when the chips are down' (from his sermon on the Sower). 'Our pocketbooks can have more to do with heaven, and also with hell, than our hymnbooks' (this from his sermon on Dives and Lazarus).

The long and short of it is this, that, in expounding the parables, we should try to combine scholarly integrity with New Testament truth and existential concern. In other words, if we must always begin by trying to discover what Jesus meant to say in his parable to those who heard it, our task will not be completed till we have made it say, '*Tua res agitur*. It concerns you, and me, and all of us.'

Note: The Parable as a Language Event

We like to contrast word with deed. But sometimes words can
do things, can change men or situations. (One thinks, for example,
of Augustine lighting on Paul's word in Rom. 13.13f., 'not in
rioting and drunkenness', hearing a voice say, 'Take and read'
and finding his whole life changed thereby.) May we think of
Jesus' parables as 'language-events', as linguistic acts, or, as
modern philosophers might call them, 'performative utterances'?
This is the view now being taken of them by a German
scholar called Ernst Fuchs. Fuchs, alas, has not the gift of
lucidity; but the reader will find an account of his approach in
the work on the parables by his pupil Eta Linnemann.[3] This we
propose to summarize, adding some illustrations of our own.

When a parable 'comes off' (as Nathan's to King David did)
it decisively alters a situation, becomes a linguistic act, *ein Tat im
Wort*. For it makes possible a new understanding between its
teller and his hearer, who is often his opponent or critic. But all
depends on the teller so using language – so drawing his hearer
into his own 'world' of thought – that he sets the issue between
them (e.g. in the Good Samaritan, 'Who is my neighbour?') in a
quite new light ('To whom can I be a neighbour?'). Indeed, even
if the parable does not succeed, all is not quite as it was before,
because the man who declines the parable's challenge (as the
Rich Young Ruler declined that of Jesus) is himself making a
decision.

A successful parable is an event in two ways: (1) It creates
a new possibility in the situation; and (2) it compels the hearer
to decide in one way or another. In his parable the teller risks
everything on the power of language. Moreover, the deeper the
opposition between the teller and his hearer, the bigger the
decision facing the hearer. And there are oppositions which go

[3] *Parables of Jesus*, London 1966, 30-33.

right down beneath a man's conscious state of mind to the depths of his very being and involve all his acts and attitudes. To such situations – and oppositions – Jesus' parables were commonly directed. (Think of the three parables in Luke 15, including the supreme one of the Prodigal Son, directed to the Pharisees' self-righteousness.)

If a parable is to strike home to its hearer, all turns on 'the moment of truth' which the teller will know how to use so that the hearer is suddenly perplexed (as Simon the Pharisee was perplexed in the narrative of Luke 7.36-50). For the man, so perplexed, truth is set against truth – the truth about the man's own existence and the truth embodied in the parable. And he must decide.

By using parables to force his hearers to decision, Jesus was giving them a chance of changing their whole existence – the chance of entering God's kingdom or, as St John puts it, finding 'eternal life'. Such a change was beyond the hearer's power to effect by his own effort. This chance of change could only come from the outside, from the parable of Jesus which struck home to him at the very deepest level of his life.

But how does all this bear on the parables today? Human existence always remains very much the same; but language (in the widest sense of the word) has a way of changing with the passage of the centuries. The parables of Jesus spoken in the first century can be transmitted to us in the twentieth; but the precise language-event cannot, simply because we do not stand in the same position and predicament as the original hearers in Galilee or Jerusalem. For us the opposition – though essentially the same – emerges at a different point. Since the language has changed, the idioms and images in the parables of Jesus (e.g. in that of the Unforgiving Servant in Matt. 18) no longer quite come home to us as they did to the first hearers. But if the language-event cannot be transmitted, it *can be made intelligible* – by careful exposition – *and it can be repeated* in proper preaching. Such preaching repeats the event experienced by the first hearers of the parable. Only such a word from the outside can change men's existence – from unbelief to faith. For, as Paul said (Rom. 10.17), 'faith comes by preaching'; and your true preacher today not only learns from Jesus how to preach but grounds his message on what Jesus did long ago when he 'risked his word' – the word of the kingdom – in parables.[4]

[4] A good parallel can be drawn between Fuchs's concept of parable as language-event and the linguistic philosopher J. L. Austin's concept of 'performative utterances' (e.g. that, at a wedding, when the minister pronounces a couple man and wife). In each case 'the issuing of the utterance is the performing of an action' (Austin). So Fuchs sees the parables as linguistic acts in which Jesus calls, promises, judges, demands, claims and gives. See A. C. Thiselton's article on this subject in *The Scottish Journal of Theology* for November 1970.

PART TWO

THE PARABLES TODAY

'The words of Christ are like a fountain which never dries up. When you draw from this fountain of wisdom, it fills up again, and the second truth you derive is fuller and more splendid than the first. Thus it is with all that proceeded from the mouth of Christ, his sayings and his parables.'
Matthias Claudius, Bishop of Turin (9th century)

4

The Coming and Growth of
the Kingdom

Five parables, four from the synoptic gospels and one from the fourth, illustrate in different ways the coming and growth of God's kingdom or reign: the Sower, the Seed growing Secretly, the Mustard Seed and the Leaven, and the Grain of Wheat.

N.B. When telling of the new age, the Old Testament prophets (Isa. 55.10f.; Jer. 31.27; Ezek. 36.9; Hos. 2.23; and Zech. 10.9) had depicted God as the great Sower. In his parables, therefore, Jesus was using a metaphor about God's action in the new age (the kingdom of God) which presumably was familiar to his hearers.

The Sower (Mark 4.3-8)

I In our industrial society so familiar are we with packaged foods that Jesus' story of a farmer and his fortunes no longer makes quite the impact on us that it once did. Once upon a time, before the coming of mechanized farming, the figure of the lone farmer hand-casting his seed was about as commonplace in the West as in the East. Some of us, who were country-bred, remember first hearing Jesus' parable about the Sower in Sunday school, even if our appreciation of it seldom went further than the 'picture' part and we never got to the 'reality' part – the truth about the kingdom of the Great Sower it was meant to teach.

Why, where, and when did Jesus tell this tale of the farmer and the varied fortunes that befell the seed he sowed?

A glance at its setting in Mark's gospel will help us to an answer. This is no townsmen's tale – it smells of the country and clearly belongs to the open-air phase of Jesus' ministry. But before Jesus had moved from the towns and made the Lake of

Galilee the *milieu* of his ministry, opposition to it had been mounting. The 'doctors of the law' had turned hostile; the Pharisees were ganging up against him, in unholy and unwonted alliance with the Herodians; he had been driven from the synagogues; there had been setbacks and discouragement; and his own family had shown misgivings about him. Small wonder that even his disciples and followers began to show signs of discouragement also. Was the great kingdom of God emprise to which Jesus had called them foredoomed to failure?

This parable was the answer to such forebodings. Perhaps, as Jesus spoke to them, there appeared on a nearby hillside a man handcasting his seed. Here was an image from real life, ready for his purpose. So the parable of the Sower was born.

Some of the sower's seed, said Jesus, fell on the footpath running through the field, only for the birds to swoop down and devour it. Some seed fell on ground where there was only a thin dusting of soil on top, and, below it, shelving rock. Up shot the young seeds; but when the sun pierced the shallow soil, it became a hot-bed where the young plants soon withered. Other seed fell on 'dirty' soil full of thorns which shot up quickly and choked the growing corn-shoots. But this was not the end of the story. Some seed fell on good ground and yielded the crop we all remember – 'some thirty, some sixty, and some a hundredfold'. If, as our experts tell us, tenfold was reckoned an average crop in Palestine, this was a bumper harvest, a harvest to gladden any farmer's heart and make him forget his losses.

Jesus' parables normally follow the rules of popular storytelling, one of which is 'the rule of end stress'. What this means is that the spotlight falls on the last item in the series – in this case, the abundant harvest. Lift, then, the whole story from the natural to the spiritual level, and its point becomes clear. 'In spite of all hazards and losses,' Jesus is saying, 'the farmer reaps a splendid crop. Even so, in spite of all frustrations and failures, God's rule advances, and his harvest exceeds expectation.' To be sure, the kingdom of God is no juggernaut; it encounters opposition and experiences failures; but it triumphs over and amid both. As unproductive pockets of soil belong to sowing, so opposition and failure belong to history and sinful human nature. But God's

kingdom belongs to the eternal realm, and what we have to
keep in view is the harvest, and not the failures.

Originally, then, on Jesus' lips the parable was a *Nil Desperan-
dum* – a ringing 'Have faith in God' – to despondent followers.
It is still a clarion-call to 'fearful saints'. Not a few Christians are
like the one who, in the spiritual doldrums, wrote:

> God's Word made a perfect beginning;
> Man spoiled the creation by sinning;
> We know that the story
> Will end in God's glory,
> But at present the other side's winning!

Doesn't the last line of that limerick describe how most of us
feel, in our black moods, about God's cause in the world? We
note how many foes are ranged against God's kingdom in the
world; we see the church's setbacks and failures; around us are
empty pews and dwindling congregations; and spiritual apathy
seems endemic in our land. It is then we must learn from Christ
that, however gloomy the outlook for the church may seem to
be, God's kingdom 'stands and grows for ever', that God's Spirit,
like a great wind, is invisibly but unceasingly at work in the
affairs of men, that the 'little flock' (Luke 12.32) which the Good
Shepherd gathered in Galilee is now the greatest society on earth,
and that the God who has already done so much for men in
Christ may be trusted to finish his work. Jesus is still saying to
us his followers, 'Have faith in God. His victory is sure.'

II   But this was not the only purpose Jesus had in mind when
he told this story about the sower and the soils. Make no mistake
about it, that circumstantial description of the various soils is
not accidental. It reflects Jesus' own experience of preaching
the gospel of the kingdom and his awareness of the need for
attentive hearing. It is therefore also a parable about hearing the
gospel – about the need for a hearing which issues in decision
and action. If it says, 'Have faith in God', it says also, 'God
depends on you'.

Let us consider this matter of how we hear the gospel. There
are various ways of hearing.[1] We can listen only with our ears,
as often happens in a polite conversation. Then it is a case of in

[1] I owe this illustration to J. W. Leitch, in his book, *The King Comes*,
London 1965, 67f.

one ear and out of the other. This suggests the seed that fell on
the footpath. Or we can listen with our minds only, as we do
to a great speaker. While he speaks, we are thrilled and profess
ourselves persuaded; but the fine impulses evoked by his words
evaporate as quickly as the moisture from the shallow soil. Or,
again we can listen – on radio or TV – to a moving appeal for
a good cause; but, well – we remember the state of our overdraft
or a friend rings up about a business deal, and the appeal goes
unanswered. The thorns have choked the young shoots. But one
day, maybe, the announcer interrupts the programme with, 'Here
is an sos message for . . .'; we hear our own name, learn that a
loved one is desperately ill; and now we hear not with our ears
only, or with minds only, but with our whole being, and
we act at once. It is a matter of life or death – a truly existential
situation.

This is the kind of hearing the gospel calls for. Momentous
issues are at stake; they concern us; we must listen and decide.

If you read the parable again, and let it put questions to you
about yourself, will they not be something like these? 'What
kind of soil am I? Am I hard soil, shallow soil, dirty soil, or good
soil?' Of course you may brush these questions aside with, 'I'm
just the way God made me, and there's nothing to be done about
it'. But this sort of fatalism is really a denial of the truth of the
gospel. The grace of God can change men, and Christian history
abounds with examples of changed men. The real truth is that
in each of us there is something of all four soils, and what the
parable says is: 'Don't let the seed fall on hard ground. Don't
be so shallow that it can't take root in you. Weed out those
thorns. Be good soil – give God his chance to do his gracious work
on you – even if it means altering your whole life.'

Yet for us, if not for those who first heard the parable, there
is a yet deeper meaning. For we who stand on the far side of the
cross and the resurrection know, as they hardly did, who the
speaker of the parable is. He is 'the Word made flesh', God's
saving purpose embodied in a man. And, by the Spirit's work,
the living Christ still confronts us with his challenge, as on our
response to it our destiny depends: 'Whoever will acknowledge
me before men,' says this Jesus, 'I will acknowledge before my
Father in heaven; and whoever disowns me before men, I will

disown him before my Father in heaven.'

What we do with Jesus and the gospel is of eternal moment. All turns on our response.

NOTE

Many modern scholars think that the 'explanation' of the Sower in Mark 4.14-20 is the early church's work. The arguments for this view are fully stated in Jeremias, *The Parables of Jesus*, 77f. The case for its substantial authenticity is well put by C. F. D. Moule in *Neotestamentica et Semitica*, 95ff. Whether the 'explanation' is the work of Jesus or of the church, it is existentially true, since it reflects the causes which still lead men to reject the gospel. And, even if after study of the problem, we decide for Jeremias rather than for Moule, finding in the 'explanation' early Christian exegesis of Jesus' story, any good sermon on the parable today would include both elements, both the Lord's teaching and the church's exposition.

The Seed Growing Secretly (Mark 4.26-29)

1 Zeal for God's glory is a wonderful and, alas, rapidly vanishing commodity in our world. But men can show what James Denney once called 'an irreligious solicitude for God'. And when such 'zealots' want to take God's work out of his hands and do it themselves, their 'solicitude' has turned 'irreligious'.

Nineteen hundred years ago, in Galilee, there were many such 'zealots', one of them 'Simon the Zealot' (as Luke calls him), numbered among Christ's chosen Twelve. Hating their Roman overlords and all their works, these Zealots stood ready to bring in God's kingdom by force and at the sword-point. It was to men of this militant temper that Jesus said, 'This is how the kingdom of God works', and went on to tell them a story about a farmer and some seed:

'A man scatters seed on the land; he goes to bed at night and gets up in the morning, and the seed sprouts and grows – how he does not know. The ground produces a crop by itself, first the blade, then the ear, then the grown crop in the ear; but as soon as the crop is ripe, he sets to work with the sickle, because the harvest-time is come.'

So Jesus links, as he likes to do, the worlds of nature and of grace (Cf. Matt. 5.45). But what is the point of comparison between the seed growing 'by itself' and the reign of God?

Observe that the farmer's work is described with the very

minimum of words. All the stress falls on the mysterious and
miraculous process of growth. Just as the earth 'spontaneously'
brings forth fruit, so God's reign comes by his power alone.
Once man plants the seed, the result is as sure, as dependable,
and as silent as the forces of nature. Stage by stage – first the
green shoot, then the spike of corn, and then the full grain
in the ear – the seed of God's kingdom grows to harvest, whether
men will or not. The point is the divine inevitability of the
whole process.

Jesus is thinking of his ministry in Galilee. Having, as God's
agent, sown the seed, he can say (like Mark Antony in the play)
'Now let it work!' Around him are hot-headed men fretful for
quick results. To them Jesus is saying, 'It's no good to shout or
to shove. The work is God's. Leave the issue to him. A new
divine force has been released in the world, and grow it will, as
surely as the sown seed, by the gracious ministry of God's sun
and rain, ripens to the harvest.'

A parable of 'agricultural grace' we might call it. When a dis-
tinguished American surgeon was asked upon what he relied
when he operated, he answered, 'medical grace'. By this he meant
that *vis medicatrix*, that recuperative and healing power in the
human body which, like the seed in the parable, works 'by
itself', and without which all his professional expertise with
the knife would be vain.

What this parable says is that, just as in nature (which is
God's creation) there is a freely-given power which man does
not make or direct, so in history there is a divine power – the
Spirit of God – which brings God's kingdom from seed to harvest.

II Now apply this truth to ourselves and our times. In our
modern world zealots who want to do God's work for him at
the sword (or should we say, bomb) point are a rare breed –
unless our young advocates of violence really, somehow, believe
they are serving God. Their place has now been taken by the
people – 'humanists' they call themselves – who think they can
dispense with such an outmoded hypothesis as belief in God,
and solve the world's problems by their own unaided expertise.

And the first thing that the parable does is to put such people
in their places when they are liable to 'get too big for their

boots'. What with all our mechanized farming and our artificial fertilizers, some men are apt to think they can do it all 'by themselves'. The plain truth is that they cannot even make a seed, and that all the tractors and combine harvesters in the world would be so much useless metal unless God 'gave the increase'.

Or take the matter out of the realm of farming and set it on a social, political or international level. Think of all the triumphs of modern technology and medicine, of automation in industry and modern means of communication, of our international organizations and our UNOS. No wonder some are naïvely persuaded that, 'by themselves', they can create 'the brave new world' of their heart's desiring. What they all forget is that the creation of such a new order depends always on dealing with that intractable thing the bible calls 'sin' and on changing men's natures. But, as God alone can create a seed and make it grow, only God can deal with 'the corruption of man's heart' and make new men. That he can do so, is the central claim of the Christian gospel, as well as the experience of countless men and women who have been changed and renewed by it.

But if the parable puts the 'do-it-yourself' men in their proper places, today it speaks primarily to those people who have not an 'irreligious' but a 'religious' solicitude for God. We are thinking of those people who want assurance that, despite all appearances to the contrary and all the prognostications of our modern Cassandras, God's great saving purpose goes forward amid the hurly-burly of history. To all such faint-hearts the parable says: 'None of us knows how a seed grows. Everyone knows that it does. And we can be just as sure that God's new order – the Kingdom – is operating in history, even if we cannot explain how it works. No gardener in his senses dreams of pulling up the seed every other day to see if it is growing. He believes that it is. Then why should we not also believe in the ongoing of God's great purpose for his world, revealed in Christ, and wait patiently (if not passively) for its fruition? We Christians believe in a living and acting God who is the Lord of history. His Spirit is even now working in all the travail of our times. Like a good farmer, let us see to it that the conditions exist in which the seed of God's gospel gets a chance to grow and, having done this, leave the rest to God.'

This is not the same thing as a facile belief in progress. Last century, bedazzled by the doctrine of evolution, men had come to believe that progress was irresistible, and that the world was going to heaven of its own momentum. Had they taken the bible more seriously, had they reckoned with 'Original Sin', they would not have indulged in such sky-blue optimism, an optimism soon to be rudely shattered by two world wars and their awful aftermaths. Yet if such easy optimism was unjustified, equally unwarranted today is the pessimism which proclaims that 'God is dead' and that the world is going to hell of its own momentum.

It is here that Christ's parable comes in to remind us that:

> Though the cause of evil prosper,
> Yet 'tis truth alone is strong,
> Though her portion be the scaffold
> And upon the throne be wrong;
> Yet that scaffold sways the future,
> And behind the dim unknown
> Standeth God within the shadow
> Keeping watch above his own.

The God 'within the shadow' is the Father of Christ. The seed which he gave his Son to sow in Galilee, which was watered by the bloody sweat of his cross, and which, by the resurrection and the coming of the Spirit, began to yield its own rich crop of saved men and women, is still growing secretly but surely to fruition; and as our God is a living and judging God, there will come a time when he 'sets to work with the sickle' because the harvest time of the ages is come.

The final question is the old one: 'Who is on the Lord's side?' Christ is still calling men to enter God's kingdom and align themselves with his purpose and:

> Once to every man and nation
> Comes the moment to decide.

Will we take our place in that kingdom of his Father which he offers us? Or will we simply go our own way and refuse his invitation? Either way, God's kingdom stands and grows for ever. Either way, his sovereignty will be exercised, in blessing or in judgment. It is for us to decide whether we will be found on the Lord's side in the battle.

Mustard Seed and Leaven (Luke 13.18-21; Mark 4.30-32)

If we accept the 'He is not here; he is risen' of the first Easter morning, the most important announcement made in the New Testament is that with which Jesus began his ministry in Galilee: 'The time has come; the kingdom of God is upon you; repent and believe the gospel' (Mark 1.14f.).

Five centuries before, Isaiah of Babylon had foretold the coming of a messenger with 'news of deliverance' who would cry aloud to Zion and the cities of Judah, 'Your God has become king!' (Isa. 40.9f.; 52.7f.) The 'good news' that the reign of God had arrived was what Israel had been waiting for centuries to hear. Now, says Jesus, the prophecy is coming true. The new order of God is dawning. Turn to God and make his good news your own.

It is always hard, at the actual time, to discern what is really going on in what is taking place. Take an instance from British history. What took place at Runnymede in 1215 was that King John, much against his will, signed the Magna Carta. When the king put pen to paper, a few of the barons present may have dimly surmised something of what was going on. But the twentieth century historian, with the benefit of hindsight, sees quite clearly that what was then being inaugurated was British parliamentary democracy as we know it.

So it is with what took place in Galilee nineteen hundred years ago. With the help of hindsight, we Christians can now see that God, through his Son, Jesus the Messiah, was setting in motion a train of events which was to issue in the rise of the new Israel, which is the church of Christ.

But in AD 28 nobody foresaw all this. All the ordinary on-looker could see was a Galilean carpenter, turned itinerant prophet and healer, who was drawing after him a motley mob of publicans and sinners. This, and on the other hand, no lack of opposition to the carpenter and his 'good news'. Already he had been turned out of the synagogues. The Jewish churchmen were saying he was in league with the devil. Even his own family wondered if he had gone out of his mind. How could this be the eternal God invading history? Possibly, even some of his close followers shared something of this doubt. Only the man who made the announcement knew what was going on in what was taking place, and in two parables he gave his hearers a pregnant hint of what it was.

Because they stand together in Luke's gospel and share the general ideas of expansion, some have said that the Mustard Seed and the Leaven are different ways of saying the same thing. But since the processes involved are different – on the one hand, growth, on the other permeation – let us study them separately, beginning with the Leaven.

When Jesus compared God's reign with leaven, he meant it was like what happened when you put a tiny bit of yeast into a batch of flour. Having watched Mary his mother do this very thing, he knew that the result would be no quiet and gradual permeation but a dynamic disturbance. Now observe the amount of meal in the story. 'Three measures of meal' (AV) is 'about half a hundredweight of flour' (NEB). Put your yeast into this amount, and you have a baking big enough to feed a hundred and fifty hungry mouths. No ordinary housewife in her senses would bake such an enormous quantity of bread. Its very vastness shows that we are dealing with no ordinary human situation but with an extraordinary divine reality – with what the sovereign power of God in action can really do. Finally note the last words of the parable – 'till all was leavened'. Is not this the very nature of leaven? It leavens the whole lump – no part of the flour can remain unaffected by it.

Now lift all this to the divine level and perceive what Jesus is implying. When the reign of God invades history, nothing can be unaffected by it. It creates a disturbance from which nothing is secure. In other words, the ferment has begun – God's great ferment – which no time or society can escape.

There is, then, in this parable a realism which is 'honest but triumphant, a realism which sees in the very facts of opposition and disturbance the present activity of God immanent in the process but not contained within it or frustrated by the process'. The disturbance which Jesus' gospel of the kingdom created is still with us. The crises and upheavals of our time often upset the simple faith of many Christians, making them doubt if the gospel is true. But if they can only be made to see that God is a living God and that in these events he is at work, that his judgments are abroad in the earth, they can be saved from cynicism and despair.

Now turn to the other parable. In the first century the mustard seed had long been a byword for the smallest thing imaginable. Jesus said to his hearers, 'Have you ever noticed that everyday miracle in the world of nature which transforms that tiny seed into a tree as tall as a horse and its rider,[2] so that the birds of the air come to roost in its branches? This miracle is about to be repeated in the spiritual world.' 'Birds of the air' was one of the rabbis' names for the Gentiles; and ever since the time of the prophet Ezekiel (see Ezek. 17.22f.; 31.6; and cf. Dan. 4.10ff., 20f.), the tree in whose shadow the wild birds made their dwelling, had been a symbol for a world-wide empire embracing all peoples. Just so, Jesus is saying, the reign of God which may now seem a thing of small importance is destined to span the earth and embrace in its sweep the Gentiles from afar. Unimaginable endings from unremarkable beginnings is the point of the parable of the Mustard Seed.

From the Galilee of AD 28 turn to the world of 1970. Nineteen centuries later there is plenty of disturbance in the earth, as there is no lack of devilry. Even among church people are those who, confronted by the giant power of evil in our society, tremble for the future of God's rule and Christ's church. It is here that these two parables, embodying as they do the assurance of Jesus, ought to put courage into all faint hearts.

Nineteen hundred years have gone by since the planting of the mustard seed and the putting-in of the leaven; and we do not yet see the final issue of God's great saving purpose declared in Christ. But the seed has in fact grown into a great tree—a church which, in spite of its unhappy divisions, now numbers more than nine hundred millions. And still God's leaven is working, working not merely in the church as it tries to match its message and ministry to a rapidly changing world, but often elsewhere in ways unrecognized by many in the turmoil and

---

[2] W. M. Thomson, *Central Palestine and Phoenicea*, 163.

confusion of our times (e.g., the revolt against racialism, the quest for world-peace, all that can be included under the name 'Christian Action').

'Ye fearful saints, fresh courage take.' God is alive today in his world. The ferment begun in Galilee is still spreading, the seed which God gave his Son to sow is still growing. If you want to see things in proper perspective, visit, as I did recently, that 3,000-year-old yew tree in the Perthshire churchyard of Fortingall, the reputed birthplace of Pontius Pilate. And, as you look at it, reflect that it antedates Pilate by ten centuries, that it had been growing there a thousand years before the mustard seed of God's kingdom began to germinate in Galilee.

So, lift up your hearts, you little-faiths! Only a small part of the scroll of history is as yet unrolled. The dawn which arose in Galilee has yet greater splendours to unfold. We are really, as William Temple said, 'the early Christians', and we have God's future before us.

The Weeds among the Wheat (Matt. 13.24-30)

Some men are more 'religious' than God himself. Every century produces them. We have them among us today. But if any sect answered this description in Christ's day, it was the Pharisees.

Their very name meant 'the separatists'; they thought of themselves as 'the holy community'; their dream was of some kind of spiritual *Apartheid*; and we know, from one of their books called *The Psalms of Solomon*, that they expected a great separating of the sinners from the saints when it should please God to send his Messiah and bring in his kingdom.

But when Jesus the Messiah did come, announcing the arrival of God's kingdom, it appeared to the Pharisees that his followers included more sinners than saints. They were incensed and indignant at the free and easy way in which Jesus was admitting all kinds of undesirables into his messianic community. 'If the kingdom of God is really here,' we can almost hear them saying, 'why has there not been a weeding out of the sinners from the saints in Israel?' In answer Jesus told a story about a farmer who woke up one day to find a lot of weeds among his grown wheat. (The weed was darnel – *lolium temulentum* its Latin name – and in the early days of growth only the expert eye can distinguish it from wheat.)

'A man,' said Jesus, 'sowed his field with good seed: but while everyone was asleep, his enemy came, sowed darnel among the wheat, and made off. (In the East enemies still play lousy tricks like this. Even in modern India the threat can still be heard, "I will sow bad seed in your field".) When the corn sprouted and began to fill out, the darnel could be seen among it. The farmer's men went to their master. "Sir," they said, "was it not good seed you sowed in your field? Then where has the darnel come from?" "This is an enemy's doing," he replied. "Then," they asked, "shall we go and gather the darnel?" "No," he answered, "in gathering it up, you might pull up the wheat at the same time. Let them both grow together till the harvest; and at the harvest time I will tell the reapers, Gather the darnel first and tie it in bundles; then collect the wheat into my barn."'

That is the story. Three centuries later, in North Africa, some strict and strait-laced Christians, declaring the church must be holy, demanded the weeding out of sinners. The reply of Augustine, the great bishop of Hippo, was to point them to Jesus' parable. Augustine had rightly seen that it is *a warning against premature weeding*. No farmer in his senses, Jesus is saying, tries to separate the weeds from the wheat while the crop is still growing. In plain prose, leave the weeding out of the bad men from the good to God at Judgment Day.

St Paul may have been commenting on Christ's parable when he wrote to the Corinthians: 'Pass no premature judgment; wait till the Lord comes. For he will bring to light what darkness hides, and disclose men's inward motives' (I Cor. 4.5).

The parable is a rebuke to our perennial temptation to be selective in our choice of where we live the religious life, where we should expect God's revelation and his blessing. William Temple once said that God was interested in a lot of things besides religion. But we men are very prone to mark out areas in which God shall operate and to remove other areas from his surveillance. So we miss the revelation that may come to us when we undertake every secular task at its full depth, and

try to do all for the glory of God. We need to heed George
Herbert's words :

> Teach me, my God and King,
> In all things Thee to see

and

> Who sweeps a room, as for Thy laws,
> Makes that, and the action fine.

But the main thrust of the parable is undoubtedly a warning
against premature weeding. This, Jesus says, is a task for God and
not for man.

Even the most amateur gardener knows what a fiky business
weeding can be. 'Is this a weed, or a flower? How do you tell
couch grass from the wheat it so often resembles?' And is not
the task still harder when we try to decide who are the saints,
and who the sinners? As the old rhyme says :

> There is so much good in the worst of us,
> And so much bad in the best of us,
> That it hardly becomes any of us
> To talk about the rest of us.

Or we may put it another way : Have you ever in your life
met a person, no matter how vicious and depraved, of whom
you could say quite certainly, 'This person is a weed and
nothing else – a rotter to the very core'?

The truth is that, if the weeding out of the sinners from
the saints were left to men, we would, as Jesus said, inevitably
rip up much good wheat along with the weeds.

Robert Burns had the Christian root of the matter in him
when he told 'the unco guid' (the rigidly righteous) of his day :

> Who made the heart, 'tis He alone
>   Decidedly can try us,
> He knows each chord, its various tone,
>   Each spring, its various bias.

Not for us mortals, then, this job of sifting out sinners from
saints! It is a task fit only for Eternal Omniscience, for the
great 'Knower of hearts' at Judgment Day.[3]

[3] The parable of the Seine-net (Matt. 13.47-50) not only warns against
premature separation but adds the assurance that it will take place later.
The business of the present hour, says Jesus in effect to his fishermen
disciples, is not to judge or sift but to catch fish of every kind.

Judgment Day? Nowadays we are told that modern man 'isn't bothering about his sins' and that he regards the notion of a final sifting of bad men from good as just a fairy tale from the bible. If this is so, it only shows that modern man presumes himself better informed on these ultimate issues than Christ himself. A true Christianity cannot dispense with the doctrine of man's final accountability to God for what he has been and done. But let it also be said that it is not for us to pronounce who will finally stand on the Saviour's right hand or his left.

Nonetheless, three things we may dare to affirm: First – and on Christ's own authority (Matt. 25.31-46) – the Last Judgment will contain surprises, with some quite unexpected – and unexpecting – people gaining a heavenly reward, and, contrariwise, some expecting people getting rude shocks.

Second: the sentence of final exclusion from God's presence will not fall on any who do not freely and deliberately pronounce it on themselves.

Third: when Christ the King comes with his sickle and his crown, if there are surprises in store, one thing will be unchanged – the Love which died to redeem us, the Love in which we have believed and hoped and endured.

Remembering these things, would not the best prayer for us all be the last verse of the last Scottish paraphrase:

> O may we stand before the Lamb
> When earth and seas have fled,
> And hear the Judge pronounce our name
> With blessings on our head?

The Grain of Wheat (John 12.24)

The parables about the coming and growth of the kingdom were uttered in Galilee before the shadow of a cross began to lengthen across the path of Jesus. But to the imagery of the sown seed and the harvest he was to come back in Jerusalem itself and in the last days of his ministry.

St John sets the parable of the Grain of Wheat just before the third and last passover of Jesus' ministry. It was evoked, he says, by the desire of some Greeks to 'interview' Jesus. For Jesus this desire was the signal that a new and wider phase in

his mission – a ministry to the Gentiles – was at hand. 'The hour
has come,' he cried, 'for the Son of Man to be glorified' (John
12.23). But he also said, almost in the same breath, 'Now is my
soul troubled' (12.27). Why? One suggestion is that at this
point the devil made a final attempt to divert him from his God-
appointed course and destiny. Why not abandon Jerusalem and
his recusant fellow-countrymen and betake himself to the bigger
world of the Gentiles? This temptation Jesus repelled. There
could be no evasion of the cross. So, prefacing it with his
doubled Amen, Jesus spoke the parable of the Grain of Wheat;
and though it occurs only in the fourth gospel, its imagery, style
and vocabulary prove it as authentic a parable of Jesus as any
in the first three gospels:[4] 'Truly, truly, I say to you, unless a
grain of wheat falls into the earth and dies, it remains alone,
but if it dies, it bears much fruit' (RSV).

Some have taken Jesus to be laying down a grim law of all
human life:

> And all through life I see a cross,
> Where sons of God give up their breath,
> There is no gain except by loss,
> There is no life except by death.

Yet, so to generalize the parable's meaning is to forget that
it was uttered in the *penumbra* of his Passion. As in his saying
about the Ransom (Mark 10.45), Jesus is thinking of the necessity
and purpose of his death. He is foretelling the rich redemptive
harvest which his completed passion will bring with it.

Once earlier (Luke 12.49f.), and with a noble impatience, he
had cried, 'I have come to send fire on the earth, and how I
wish it were already kindled! But I have a baptism to undergo,
and how constricted I am until the ordeal is over!' Before the
fire of the gospel can blaze, the bearer of the gospel must die.
His baptism in blood is his necessary initiation into a fuller
and freer activity where (as the centurion Longinus said in
Masefield's play) he 'will be let loose in the world where neither
Roman nor Jew can stop his truth'.

This, though the metaphor is different, is essentially what
Jesus says in his parable. His death is the inescapable condition
of his ministry becoming greatly fruitful in the wider world.

[4] See my *According to John*, London 1968, 83f.

If it is to yield its rich crop, the planted seed must be watered by the bloody sweat of his passion.

Three centuries before Christ a Greek named Archimedes had said, 'Give me a proper place to stand on, and I will move the world'. 'Give me a cross to hang on,' said Jesus (John 12.32), 'and I will draw all men to myself.'

Has not the Lord's presence been vindicated? 'The Cross of Christ,' wrote Mrs Hamilton King, 'is more to us than all his miracles.' 'Christ died on the Tree,' Carlyle told Emerson, as they walked the Galloway moors together, 'that built Dunscore Kirk yonder.'

But if the parable concerns the necessity and purpose of Christ's death, his saying which follows it carries its corollary for every true follower of his: 'The man who loves himself is lost' (John 12.25). Here was something new. 'In all Greek thought,' wrote William Temple,[5] 'there is no appreciation of the excellence of self-sacrifice ... This is the point – the vital point – where the ethics of the Gospel leaves the ethics of Greek philosophy far behind.'

Self-sacrifice, says Jesus, is the way to self-fulfilment. The Christian dies to live. This, as Paul knew (I Cor. 4.7-12), is a law of the Christian life at its deepest and best. And the blood of the martyrs, from Stephen to Bonhoeffer, is ever the seed of the church.

[5] *Readings in St John's Gospel*, London 1945, 196.

5

The Grace of the Kingdom

Seven parables – the Two Debtors, the Lost Sheep and the Lost Coin, the Waiting Father, the Pharisee and the Tax-collector, the Unforgiving Debtor, and the Good Employer – declare 'the extravagant goodness of God' to sinners in bringing his kingdom. Most of these parables are Jesus' ripostes to the scribes and Pharisees who had criticized him for opening the gates of the kingdom to outcasts and sinners. In one way or another, they all set forth 'the wideness of God's mercy' and represent the polemics of the divine love incarnate in Jesus and his mission to the despised and disinherited. No group of parables takes us nearer to the very heart of Jesus' 'good news'.

The Two Debtors (Luke 7.36-50)

Reinhold Niebuhr somewhere observes that much evil is done in the world by 'good people who do not know that they are not good'. People like Simon the Pharisee.

Here was a pious and prosperous Jewish churchman. Being curious to know more about the young prophet Jesus of Nazareth, he had invited him to dinner. While the meal was in progress, suddenly into the dining room there came, uninvited, 'a woman with a bad name in the town' – a well-known prostitute. Bearing an alabaster bottle of perfume, she made a bee-line for Simon's guest. But before she could remove the stopper from her bottle, her tears began to fall on Jesus' feet. Forgetting it was something a respectable woman would never do before men, she let down her hair to wipe them away, while she covered Jesus' feet with kisses and poured her perfume on them.

In all this Simon's face was a study in shocked horror; but his guest, quite unabashed and unprotesting, accepted the woman's homage.

What lay behind her extraordinary demonstration of devotion to Jesus which horrified his host? The only convincing explanation is that Jesus had met the woman before and, by his assurance of God's love for sinners, had brought her to a true repentance.[1]

But pious, prissy Simon cannot see it this way. All he can see is the sort of woman who has invaded his dining room; all he can mutter is 'If this man were really a prophet, he would know what kind of woman is touching him'.

'Simon,' said Jesus, reading his thoughts, 'I have something to say to you.'

A parable, according to P. G. Wodehouse's definition, is one of those biblical stories which at first sounds like a pleasant yarn, but keeps something up its sleeve which suddenly pops up and knocks you flat. The one Jesus now told Simon was like this. Its aim was to make Simon see the naked truth about himself and about the woman.

'There were two debtors,' said Jesus, 'one owed fifty pounds, the other five. When they had nothing to pay with, the money-lender let them both off. Now (said Jesus to Simon), which of the two, do you think, will love his creditor more, will feel more grateful to him?'

Here stop and note what a truly extraordinary creditor this is. A creditor who lets both his debtors off and go scot-free! This is not the way earthly moneylenders behave – unless they have gone out of their minds. Clearly Jesus is thinking of the supreme Creditor – of God, to whom he bade us pray, 'Forgive us our debts'. 'Can't you see, Simon,' he is saying, 'that this woman's love shows her gratitude to God for his wonderful forgiveness to her? In wronging both her and me you are missing God's best gift.'

But Simon is quite unaware that the story is meant for him-

---

[1] 'Was it hysterics, the weakness of a breaking wave?' asks James Denney. And he answers, 'No, it was not hysterics. It was regeneration' (*The Christian Doctrine of Reconciliation*, London 1917, 14). Cf. also Jeremias, *The Parables of Jesus*, 126f.

self. 'You ask me,' he says, 'who will be more grateful. Why, of course, the debtor who was let off most.'

'How right you are,' replies Jesus. Then, turning to the woman, he says: 'Simon, do you see this woman?' This was not a casual question. 'This woman' was precisely what Simon could not see. All he could see was the sort of woman she was. So Jesus must strike the blindness from his soul and show Simon to himself. 'When I came into your dining room,' he goes on, 'you gave me no kiss. This woman whom you despise has never ceased to kiss my feet. You gave me no water to wash my feet. This woman has washed them with her tears. You gave me no oil for my head. This woman has anointed my feet with costly perfume.'

For Jesus these three little courtesies – all characteristically Oriental – were far from trivial. They revealed the woman, just as Simon's omission of them revealed Simon and his desiccated and self-righteous soul. Though he was 'not good' in God's sight, Simon showed no consciousness of sin; but sin, sin flagrant and incarnate, he could see in the woman. For her part, the woman could only feel and express her overwhelming debt to Jesus for the forgiveness of her sins.

'And so I tell you,' concluded Jesus, 'her great love proves that her many sins have been forgiven by God.'

Does not this story rebuke the Pharisee who still lurks, hidden but very much alive, in many of us? Does it not castigate our complacency with ourselves and our quickness to classify and condemn other people?

'Why,' said Jesus on another occasion, 'why do you observe the splinter in your brother's eye and never notice the plank in your own eye? How dare you say to your brother "let me take the splinter out of your eye" when all the time there is a plank in your own?'

We can all see and condemn wickedness in other people. 'Yes,' commented T. W. Manson[2] grimly, and went on: 'The contemplation of human folly and sin, with the aid of a looking-glass, is a less congenial occupation, but very salutary.' If many of us were as really concerned with the reformation of others

---

[2] *The Sayings of Jesus*, London 1949, 58.

as we profess to be, we should begin with the blackguard under our own bonnet.

Robert Burns once sighed:

> O wad some Pow'r the giftie gie us
> To see oursels as others see us,
> It wad frae many a blunder free us
> And foolish notion.

But would it not be better still to see ourselves as Jesus, as God himself, sees us?

So we come back to Jesus' question to Simon, 'Do you see this woman?' Simon liked to arrange people in classes; and for him this woman's class was 'sinner'. And having established her class, he knew how she should be treated. Jesus did not classify people this way. He saw individual men and women in their situations and sin. He was not interested in what class they belonged to, but in who they were. He was concerned with them as persons, as potential children of his heavenly Father. And the clear implication of this wonderful story is that some whom we account Hell-deserving sinners may be nearer to God than many a good churchman or churchwoman. It makes us think – or it ought to.

Why, according to Jesus, do people like this woman 'go first into God's kingdom' (Matt. 21.31)? It is because no pride, no self-respect hinders them from seeing Jesus. The sad fact is that they so rarely see Jesus' kind of love in us his followers. If this is ever to happen, then the love of God shown in Jesus, must first burn up our own pride, our morality, our religion, just as it melted the dark despair in that woman's life.

The question Christ still puts to us is this: 'How do you see and treat people – as persons, or as "sorts of persons" – as sorts of persons to be categorized and condemned, or as persons to be pitied and helped?' For, as Jesus is the revealer of the unseen Father (John 14.8), so God, to whom all hearts are open, sees people in the way Jesus did – as persons, as persons who, though sinners, can be saved and become redeemed children of God.

And so must everyone of us see persons, who aspires to have 'the mind of Christ'.

Lost Sheep and the Lost Coin (Luke 15.1-10)

Many of the supreme sayings in history – like Luther's *'Ich kann nicht anders* – I can no other', at Worms – have been replies extorted from the speaker in face of criticism and condemnation.

When Jesus told the parables of the Lost Sheep and the Lost Coin (not to mention the Prodigal Son), he was under heavy fire from the scribes and Pharisees (Luke 15.1f.). These respectable churchmen were shocked to see how Jesus – who, some were whispering, was the long-expected Messiah – kept open house and table for reprobates and bad characters. Perhaps we may understand their feelings if we try to picture Jesus today leaving some 'swell' West-end church to sit down at table in an East-end café with a bunch of local ne'er-do-wells and social 'drop-outs'. 'This fellow,' they complained, 'plays host to notorious sinners and eats with them.'

'Two are better than one,' said the old Preacher (Eccl. 4.9). It was often Jesus' way to use two parables instead of one, in order to make sure his point was properly taken. These two parables form such a pair. Their general shape is the same – first, the bitterness of loss, then the anxious search, and finally the jubilation of discovery. But if they are twins, they are not identical twins, for one is about a man, and the other about a woman. Nonetheless, they drive home the same essential truth – the endless trouble people will take to recover their lost property and the joy they experience when they find it. 'God,' says Jesus, 'is like that, and this is why you find me among the down-and-outs.'

The parables, then, were Jesus' justification of his mission to the last, the least and the lost. 'If you ask me why I am concerned with these social outcasts, my answer is, Because they are God's concern and therefore mine.'

'Imagine,' he says, 'a shepherd tending a hundred sheep in some hill pasture when, one evening as he counts them, he finds one missing. Nibbling its way from one green tuft to another the animal has wandered through some hole in a dyke, to end up lost and likely to perish. At once the shepherd acts as any true man should. Leaving the rest of his flock in the care of a fellow shepherd, off he goes in search of the lost sheep till he finds it. Picture his joy then (says Jesus) as he lifts it on his shoulders and goes back to call his friends together. "Rejoice with me, for I have found the lost one." '

'Or think,' says Jesus, 'of a humble housewife who loses one day – probably in the straw of a dark corner in her windowless room – a silver coin which possibly formed part of her necklace. At once she lights a lamp, and with her twig-broom sweeps every nook and cranny, till at last the tinkle of the coin on the stone floor signals the end of her search. So she calls her friends and neighbours together. "Let's have a celebration," she says, "for I have found that precious coin of mine." '

Jesus is saying to his critics: 'What person among you, if he loses a sheep or a precious coin, will not search unweariedly for it, and break out into rejoicing when he finds it? Just so, God goes searching for his lost children and is overjoyed when he recovers them. That is what the Almighty is like, and this is why, as his Agent, I act as I do.'

When Jesus says, in the story of the lost sheep, 'There will be greater joy in heaven', he means 'God will be gladder – gladder over one sinner who repents than over ninety-nine virtuous people who do not need to repent – who have committed no gross sin.'

'Note,' says G. B. Caird,[3] 'with what confidence Jesus speaks of things that happen in heaven. He knows God well enough to know what will make him happy.'

That is a Christian scholar's comment. But even a non-Christian Jew like Claude Montefiore[4] cannot withhold his meed of praise for this story of the shepherd searching for his lost sheep. 'Here,' he says, 'is a new figure which has never ceased to play its great part in the moral and religious development of the world.'

Montefiore is right. Some have said that it is 'the redemptive joy of God' which is the point of this parable. But surely it is not so much the joy of the penitent sinner – though this also is true – as the divine love which goes out to seek the sinner before he repents. This is precisely what Jesus did. Did he not

---

[3] *St Luke*, London 1968, 181.
[4] *The Synoptic Gospels*, II. 520f.

seek out and consort with the outcasts – sitting where they sat,
eating where they ate – not because he was moved by some
noble humanitarian impulse, but because he knew he was ful-
filling God's will and purpose? 'God wills the restoration of the
outcast,' he means, 'and this is why I am, as some of you nick-
name me, "the Sinners' Friend".'

Now, as St John the Seer would say, hear what the Spirit is
saying to us through these parables today.

First (and, if you like, theologically): If you feel, as so many
people do today, lost and bewildered amid the immensities of
this mysterious universe, let these parables assure you, on
Christ's authority, that behind the immensities reigns One
who cares for you, and to whom you are as precious as a lost
ornament to a woman or a lost sheep to a shepherd. And the
proof of it is the fact that God has sent his only Son into the
world to seek and save you – save you from your lostness and
make you sons and daughters in his Father's house with its many
rooms.

The second and more practical thing is this. You and I are
members of Christ's church. Do we realize what this means?
We are limbs in Christ's *working* Body in the world. While he
was on earth, our Lord was the Servant Messiah; and now the
church is the organism through which the risen and regnant
Lord continues his saving ministry among men.

The parables we have been studying were originally Jesus'
own justification, to his critics, of his mission, based on the will
of God. That will of God has not changed with the passage of
nineteen centuries. Still God wills the reclamation of the outcasts. If it is to be true to the mind of Christ, the church today
must be the caring church. William Temple said that the church
ought to be the institution which exists primarily for the
benefit of non-members. And he was right. Are we not then
called by our Lord to seek out and succour the lost men and
women in the 'mixed-up moral-immoral, devil-may-care society'
of our time? Will not the church today be true to its divine
Lord if it becomes more and more what William Booth designed
his Army to be – 'soldiers of pity' – a body of men and women
dedicated in Christ's name, to rescuing and reclaiming the lost
children of God?

The Waiting Father (Luke 15.11-32)

By common consent this is 'the pearl among the parables'. Some would call it the greatest short story ever told. Judging it as a work of imaginative art, Robert Bridges declared it 'a perfectly flawless piece of work'. Small wonder that down the centuries it has inspired Rembrandt's pencil, the music of Debussy, a moving poem by John Masefield, and even choreographical treatment by the Sadler's Wells ballet.

But how do we interpret it?

Great scholars (like Jeremias) have warned us against allegorizing it. They have told us that we should not seek to identify the chief *dramatis personae* – the father and his two sons. But have we any option? All three plainly have a representational significance; and the most natural interpretation of the parable – the only one which makes sense of it – is that which identifies the father with God, the younger son with the publicans and sinners whom Jesus befriended, and the elder son with the scribes and Pharisees who criticized him for doing so. In the parable, therefore, God, by the lips of Jesus, declares his free forgiveness for the penitent sinner, while at the same time gently rebuking the self-righteous Pharisees.

If this is a true reading of the parable, the old name for it is misleading. Some have proposed to re-name it the story of 'the Two Sons'. There is some force in this, for if the younger son was lost in the 'far country', the elder was equally lost behind a barricade of self-righteousness. (T. W. Manson said the younger son wanted to have an overdraft from his father, the elder to open a deposit account, and of the two the latter was the deadlier sin.) But the title 'the Two Sons' also gets the parable out of focus, for the chief character in it is neither of the sons but the father. Right up to the very last scene – his meeting with the elder brother – the father broods over the whole story. Call it then, as Jeremias does, the parable of 'the Father's love', or entitle it, as Thielicke does, 'the Waiting Father'. It does not really matter, for the father 'waits' because he loves, and the father means God.

Now take a further step. Jesus' parables, as we have seen, are generally stories from real life. This is one of the things

which distinguish them from allegories which have a way of
straying into some 'Never Never Land'. To this rule our parable
seems no exception. They had prodigal sons in Jesus' day. We
still have them – the young men (and women) who say, 'Why
can't I get away from parental control for a bit – the old man
(or the old woman) is getting on my nerves – and see life and
sow my wild oats before settling down?' In the same way every
generation has its own 'far country', and one of its modern
names is 'Hippie Land'.

Yes, but if this is a story from real life, it is far more. Adolf
Jülicher and others have taken Jesus to be saying in this parable,
'This is how an earthly father would treat his returning prodigal.
And will not the Good Father above?' But question: is this in
fact how ordinary human fathers generally welcome home their
returning prodigals? Do they really run to meet them, embrace
and kiss them, load them with new clothes and expensive
presents, and reward them with a barbecue and a ball?

You may have heard of the modern prodigal who, on turning
up in the far country of a neighbouring parish, was advised by
the local minister to 'go back home and his father would kill
the fatted calf for him'. The prodigal did so, and months after,
meeting the minister again, was asked hopefully, 'Well, and
did he kill the fatted calf for you?' 'No,' was the rueful reply,
'but he nearly killed the prodigal son.'

Who will deny that it often happens so in real life, even in
this 'permissive age'?

The point is that Jesus' story is larger than life. The father of
the prodigal is not an ordinary father but a quite extraordinary
one. What Jesus is here depicting is the extravagant love of
God – his sheer grace – to undeserving men, the God who (as
Paul was to describe him) 'acquits guilty men'.

Yet if our ears are properly attuned, we may hear more in the
parable than this. We have stressed the background of Messianic
authority from which Jesus' parables proceed, and declared that
some contain implicit Christology – veiled hints of who he knew
himself to be. This parable is an example. It is not only a story
about the grace of God; it is a veiled hint that its teller is acting
for God, making God's grace and goodness real to me. 'What
I am doing,' Jesus says in effect, 'represents God's nature and

will. In my ministry God's love for the penitent sinner is being actualized.' So the parable, without making any explicit Christological claim, is a veiled assertion of Jesus' authority. He is claiming to be God's agent and envoy, to be acting in God's stead.

Who is this, we may well ask, who knows himself to be the sheer goodness and grace of God in Galilean flesh and blood?

At this point, just as we are bringing Christ into his own parable, we may almost hear Jülicher and Liberal theologians like him entering their protest: 'But there is no cross in the parable. It has no room for a mediator between God and the sinner. Not only does it proclaim the free forgiveness of God for the penitent, but it seems to suggest that the sinner can repent unaided. Is not this the real heart of Jesus' gospel, and is not the doctrine that "Christ died for our sins" (I Cor. 15.3) just a mystification introduced into Jesus' simple gospel by Paul and later theologians?'

To this objection we might reply that any true doctrine of the Atonement must be based on the whole set of facts presented by the ministry, death and resurrection of Jesus and on the experience of countless Christians down the centuries who have found forgiveness in 'the healing cross'. But here it is more relevant to remember Jülicher's own ruling that a parable makes one point, and we must not expect to find in it Jesus' whole gospel. In fact, the parables form a kind of running commentary on a great campaign – the campaign of the kingdom of God against the dominion of evil – which took Jesus to the cross. Jesus did not utter his full purpose – which was God's purpose – in this or indeed in any other parable. He uttered it in the very last thing he ever did, the end which crowned his work, and of which (St John tells us) he cried in triumph, 'It is finished!' 'The work is done!' For there came a time when words – even supreme parables like this one – were of no avail, when only a deed could effect what God had sent him to do. That deed was the cross on which, by his Father's appointing, he gave his life 'as a ransom for many' (Mark 10.45) and thereby reconciled a prodigal race to God.

Our parable speaks of the grace of God to sinners. The Cross *is* that grace of God in final and decisive action, God's own great parable acted out in the stuff of human history, a parable whose meaning Paul took when he said, 'God demonstrates his love towards us, in that while we were yet sinners Christ died for us' (Rom. 5.8).

And now, in the ending, we must face the question of how we are to 'put across' the truth of the parable to modern man.

We may of course begin by saying that in it God, through Jesus, declares his forgiveness for the penitent sinner (while at the same time gently rebuking the self-righteous), and that, as God is unchanging, that declaration and that rebuke are time-less – as true today as when Jesus spoke the parable. But how do we make this truth 'existential', make it fit modern man's spiritual predicament?

Some (like G. V. Jones) have seen in the parable an image of our human experience. We can read the whole story in the first person and say, 'Yes, that describes me.' The parable then becomes a description of modern man's existence in the world – how he chooses freedom only, like the prodigal, to encounter loneliness and 'lostness', so that, when he comes to his senses, he realizes that his true destiny lies in life in community. Read-ing the parable this way, you may see in it a little drama in three acts – the first, Freedom and Estrangement, the second, Longing and Return, and the third, Anguish and Reconciliation. The result is a kind of modern existential Pilgrim's Progress – one thinks of somebody like Edwin Muir, the Scottish poet – whose theme can be summed up in T. S. Eliot's lines:[5]

> The end of all our exploring
> Will be to arrive where we started,
> And to know the place for the first time.

Now if this way of reading the parable proves a means of grace to some forwandered modern man, and leads him to find a mean-ing in life and his true destiny in community, the last thing we should do is to condemn it as valueless, more especially if the community should turn out to be the community of Christ – the church.

But this reading of it is purely existential, not evangelical; and any true treatment of the parable must be *both* – must not only speak to man today in his spiritual *malaise* but embody also the Good News of God.

[5] *Four Quarters*, 'Little Gidding'.

Therefore let the younger son stand for all those today who, fed up with 'the Establishment' and impatient of 'law and order' in every form, rebel against them and resolve to have their fling. Likewise, let the elder son represent all the unadventurous, conventional Christians who turn a cold, disliking eye on all their contemporaries with rebellious instincts and anarchical leanings.

To those stay-at-home Christians – 'those dull, prissy paragons' as the prodigals might call them – who complain that they have always done what they should but have never had any 'bright lights' in their lives, the Father of the parable is saying, 'Son, you are always with me, and all that is mine is yours'. In other words, if you happen to be in the elder son's shoes, give God thanks every day for the blessings you so lightly take for granted, and be grateful that you have escaped the heartache and hopelessness of your prodigal contemporaries.

And to the modern prodigals the Father (who is God) is saying: 'You have chosen freedom, and I did not stop you. All the time you have been in the far country I have been worrying about you. And I am still waiting to welcome you home.'

For the abiding truth of Christ's greatest parable is that behind the drift and destiny of human affairs, and brooding over them in infinite compassion, is a holy and eternal Father, and that, as Augustine, the greatest returned prodigal of them all, said, 'our hearts will never find rest until they find it in him'.

So the last secret of the parable is this:[6] 'There is a homecoming for us all, because there is a home.' The door of the kingdom which leads to the Father's House with its many rooms (John 14.6), still stands open: as there is one who has died and risen to open it and who still says, 'I am the real and living way to the Father' (John 14.6). The existential question is, 'Do we want to come home?' For, as P. T. Forsyth[7] puts it, 'we are all predestined in love to life, sooner or later – *if we will*'.

---

[6] H. Thielicke, *The Waiting Father*, London 1960, 29.
[7] *This Life and the Next*, London 1946, 16.

The Pharisee and the Publican (Luke 18.9-14)[8]

Real holiness, when you find it in man or woman – in a Saint Margaret or a Pope John – is a beautiful and Godlike quality, moving even pagan men to wonder. But when holiness turns to 'holier-than-thou-ness', the best turns to the worst, righteousness to self-righteousness, holy ones into 'Holy Willies'. And these are an abomination to holy God and to every honest man.

Study the New Testament and you will see that both our Lord and St Paul agree that 'none are so far from God as the self-righteous'. For when a man knows that he is righteous, the odds are that he is not. Spurgeon once said that he thought a certain man in his congregation the holiest man he had ever known – till the man told him so himself!

To rebuke those who 'were sure of their own goodness', Jesus told the story of the Pharisee and the Publican.

The Pharisees were the really religious people in Israel. The trouble was that in many cases their religion had gone bad on them. They had turned into self-righteous humbugs holding themselves aloof from the rabble who, in their view, did not properly keep the Ten Commandments and all the other rules and regulations of the Law of Moses.

Among these they included the 'publicans' or tax-collectors. They were the men who ingathered the imperial taxes for their Roman overlords and made a handsome 'cut' for themselves in the process. Every right-thinking Pharisee regarded them as rogues and renegades.

But the Pharisee and the Tax-collector in Jesus' story are really timeless characters. Every age produces their like, and we might even catch an occasional glimpse of them in the mirror.

Look first at the contrast between the two men. Try to picture the Pharisee swaggering up the Temple steps into the Divine Presence. He glowers at the tax-collector – what right has that wretch to be there at all? And then, 'taking up his stance by himself',[9] – aloof from the common herd – he proceeds to pour the tale of his own righteousness into the ear of the omniscient God.

How differently the tax-collector goes into the Divine

---

[8] Verse 14b is a 'floating' saying of Jesus found also in Matt. 23.13 and Luke 14.11. We should disregard it when interpreting the parable.

[9] Reading, with Codex Bezae, *statheis kath' heauton*.

Presence! He stands 'afar off', with his eyes fixed not on heaven but on earth; and he keeps beating his breast, overwhelmed by the sense of his own distance from God. Not a syllable has he to say in criticism of his neighbours – only seven short words which echo the greatest of the penitential psalms (Ps. 51.1). Yet these seven words reveal the whole man as on a black night a flash of sheet lightning will reveal a landscape.

Now contrast the men's prayers. The Pharisee's is really a catalogue of negative virtues plus what theologians have called 'works of supererogation' – that is, extra acts of piety calculated to establish a man's claim on God's favour.

He begins by thanking God that he is not like the rest of men – robbers, swindlers, adulterers, or, for that matter, like the tax-collector. Then he proceeds to rehearse his extra merits in the Almighty's ear. Twice a week – on Mondays and Thursdays – he fasts. Here he is telling God that he does more than is necessary, for the only fast mandatory on a Jew fell once a year on the Day of Atonement. But, besides fasting, he gives God ten per cent of all he gets. This also goes beyond what was required of a good Jew. Probably he told God a good deal more about himself; for the whole burden of his prayer is himself, and pulsating through it you can hear that horrid little pronoun 'I'.

Very different is the tax-collector's prayer. No question of merits in his case. He is a rotter, and he knows it. He has seen his own sinfulness against the burning holiness of God, and all he can say is, 'God, be merciful to me, a sinner.' Someone has said that when the heart is stirred it speaks in telegrams. The tax-collector's prayer is like that.

You can tell a man's character from the books he reads or the friends he keeps. But, if you could hear them, nothing would reveal a man more than the prayers he makes. The whole Pharisee comes out in his – his snobbery, his sanctimony, his mawkish self-esteem. Mind you, the things of which he brags are not bad things. He goes to synagogue on Sabbath. He gives ten per cent of his income for religious purposes. His private life is probably above suspicion. The trouble is that he knows his own goodness. The good man has become what the Scots call 'the unco guid'.

It would be wrong to whitewash the tax-collector. He has

faults aplenty. He lives by what we call 'graft'. By patriotic standards he is a traitor. Probably his attendance at synagogue is far from what it might be. Doubtless his private life contains some guilty secrets. But he knows it – knows that he is a sinner, that the holy God hates sin, and he casts himself on the Everlasting Mercy imploring only forgiveness.

> Two men went up to pray. O rather say,
> One went to brag – the other went to pray.[10]

Look last at the answers which the two prayers received. What we nowadays call 'the punch line' comes in the last sentence of the parable. 'It was this man – the tax-collector,' said Jesus, 'and not the other, who went home acquitted of his sins.'[11]

The tax-collector was accepted and forgiven by God; the Pharisee was not. In fact, his prayer did him harm. The man who is as good as he wishes to be will get worse, not better. This was the Pharisee's condition. His prayer was not heard.

George Meredith once wrote :

> Who rises from his prayer a better man,
> His prayer is answered.

The tax-collector's prayer was answered. He 'rose a better man', not because he had been instantly transformed into a spotless saint but because he knew that God had forgiven his sins.

When the tax-collector prayed, 'God be merciful to me a sinner,' said Kierkegaard, 'it showed his awareness of being in danger.' And is not this the abiding Word of God that Jesus speaks to us through this parable? The Pharisees of Jesus' day may long be dust, but their 'soul' – their spirit and temper – 'goes marching on', – even in the church. What we call 'Pharisaism' is still a besetting sin of our religion. The selfish ego of the Pharisee dies hard in us; we still reproduce in our acts and attitudes that unlovely self-righteousness which Jesus pilloried in his parable; we show little 'awareness of being in danger'. And that goes not only for the ultra pious who are quite sure they

[10] Richard Crashaw, 'Steps to the Temple'.
[11] 'Acquitted of his sins.' Lit. 'justified' (Greek : *dedikaiomenos*). This is Jesus speaking, not Paul. It is a reminder that Paul's doctrine of justification by God's grace through faith has its roots in Jesus' teaching. See my *Gospel according to St Paul*, London 1966, 84-86.

are 'saved' but for all church people who are at ease in their own little Zions. May God, of his mercy, jolt us all out of our spiritual self-complacency!

The Unforgiving Debtor (Matt. 18.23-35)

1 When General Oglethorpe said to John Wesley, 'I never forgive', Wesley replied, 'Then I hope, sir, you never sin.' Wesley must have been remembering, among other sayings of Jesus, a story he once told about an unforgiving debtor.

A king (hereinafter called 'the master') held an accounting with his servants who should be regarded not as slaves but as officials in the royal establishment. The first to appear before him was a high-ranking servant, whose debt 'ran into millions'. In order to recoup himself, the master decided to follow the usual legal procedure by selling the man, his wife, his children, and all he had in the market. Whereupon the servant prostrated himself before the master: 'Only be patient with me, and I will pay you in full.' The master's response must have exceeded his wildest hopes, for he not only released the servant but let him off his whole enormous debt.

But no sooner had that servant gone out than he met a fellow-servant – a junior colleague – who owed him 'a few pounds'. With his hands on his throat, he demanded, 'Pay me what you owe.' The underling fell at his feet: 'Be patient and I will repay you.' But, this time, the response was a blank refusal. 'The big debtor' (as we may call him) promptly had the 'little debtor' jailed till he should pay his debt.

When the other servants heard what had happened, off they went in wrath to tell the whole story to the master. To their surprised delight, the master fully shared their indignation. Recalling the big debtor, he said, 'You scoundrel! I remitted your vast debt when you appealed to me. Were you not solemnly bound to show your fellow-servant the same pity as I showed you?' And he condemned him to torture till he should pay his debt in full. (The harshness of the story's ending should not be hardened into any doctrine of eternal punishment.)

'This,' said Jesus, 'is how my heavenly Father will deal with you, unless you forgive each other not merely with your lips but from your hearts.'

II Now set the tale in its original context. At the heart of the good news of the kingdom of God which Jesus came proclaiming was the assurance of divine forgiveness – a forgiveness which Jesus himself mediated to sinful men and women (Mark 2.10; Luke 7.36-50). And what they had received he expected them to give. Freely they had received God's forgiveness, therefore freely they should forgive their fellow-men. The man who forgives, he taught, will be dealt with on the basis of forgiveness, but he who refuses to forgive can expect nothing but stern judgment from God.

This is the main lesson which the parable drives home. Yet there is something else in it which is worth noting. The big debtor's debt 'ran into millions', the man he had jailed owed him 'only a few pounds'. Is not this Jesus' way of reminding us that the debt others owe us is but a drop in the bucket compared with the ocean of our own indebtedness to God?

III What has this story, told centuries ago to long-dead listeners, to say to us today?

Revenge is natural and, proverbially, 'sweet'. ('Yes,' commented Sir Walter Scott, 'the sweetest morsel ever cooked in hell.') Real forgiveness – full forgiveness from the heart – is never easy, even for those who know themselves sinners forgiven by God for Christ's sake. So the parable warns us that 'even the saved are not safe', for the simple reason that the existence in a Christian of a harsh and unforgiving spirit sets him right back where he was before he became one.

Once in his South Sea Island home R. L. Stevenson, conducting family worship, rose suddenly in the middle of the Lord's Prayer and left the room. To his wife who followed, thinking he had been taken ill, and asking the reason why he had left, he replied, 'Because I am not fit today to pray the Lord's Prayer'.

But Jesus' story has even deeper things to suggest about justice, mercy – and God.

When, for example, we hear the sentence pronounced on the unforgiving debtor, we say, 'Serve the rascal right! He got what he deserved'. Thus the parable compels us to agree with the master's verdict on him. Our agreement, however, is no simple matter of course; for the unfortunate debtor behaved as we do ourselves every day. Taking his stand on the principle of justice, he sought to recover his debt in accordance with the law. Why then do we judge his conduct so inexcusable?

The answer lies in the contrast between mercy received and un-mercy shown. 'Be merciful,' said Jesus to his disciples, 'even as your Father is merciful' (Luke 6.36); and for him 'the quality of mercy', so far from being something only to be granted on single and exceptional occasions, had the nature of an *ordinance*, that is, something providentially written into the moral constitution of things – as justice is an ordinance.

Of course we normally take a very different view of mercy. We think of it as the momentary renouncing of what we could claim by right – as 'an exception to the rule', the rule of justice. But once the truth of Christ's parable comes home to us, does not mercy itself take on the nature of an ordinance? No longer an exception, mercy becomes the norm, with any action falling short of it a grievous moral failure. Put otherwise, in the parable mercy confronts us as a *demand*, and there would seem to be such a thing as justice only so far as mercy allows it.

To this a man may retort, 'But justice – it's as natural as the sun in the sky'. 'Is it really?' we can almost hear Jesus demurring, 'Is it not mercy?' Jesus is appealing to the nature of God. He is challenging us to 'risk our lives on mercy'[12] because it is God's way and nature. To be sure, only experience can show us that mercy is the way in which God orders his world. On the other hand, that experience can be ours, only if we will take the risk and make this venture of faith. Yet have we any alternative as Christians? The risk must be taken, or we will be false to 'the truth as it is in Jesus'.

So the story of the unforgiving debtor faces us with the searching question, 'Are you ready to stake your lives on mercy as belonging to the last reality in the universe – as being the very nature of God himself?'

[12] See Eta Linnemann's *Parables of Jesus*, 111-13, to which I am here deeply indebted.

The Good Employer (Matt. 20.1-15)

Here is a gospel story which recalls the old 'Feeing Fairs' in
our land, where farm-workers, keen on a change, or wanting
employment, would meet their potential employers. A bargain
would be struck, conditions agreed, and a wage fixed. But though
the setting of the parable is the market-place – the employment
exchange of Jesus' day – is it really a story about what is a
'just wage' or is it perhaps something profounder – a story about
the goodness of God?

The short answer is: The grumblers in the tale are the
Pharisees of Jesus' day. It is their jealousy which Jesus exposes,
while he proclaims the true nature of God. The parable is therefore, as C. L. Mitton has said, 'one of the great affirmations in
the teaching of Jesus of the gospel of God's grace'.

Listen to the story again. It was autumn in Palestine and time
to gather in the grapes. Since the rainy season was at hand,
speed was of the very essence, with the more hands the better.
So one morning at 6 a.m. the owner of the estate (whom for
short we will call the Employer) went out to engage harvesters.
Finding some, he agreed to pay them a pound[13] a day, and the
first squad 'got down to it'. About 9 a.m., coming on some idle
men in the market-place, the Employer bade them join the first
lot, promising them 'a fair wage'. So they began to work. At
noon and again at 3 p.m. he did likewise. Then, at about 5 p.m.,
an hour before sunset, meeting some more unemployed, he said,
'Go and join the others in my vineyard'.

But the really surprising thing happened an hour later when
falling darkness put an end to all work. The Jewish Law said,
'You shall not keep back a hired man's wages till next morning'
(Lev. 19.13). So the Employer said to his man of business, 'Call
the workers together and pay them their wages, beginning with
the last arrivals and ending with the first'.[14]

When the last-comers stepped forward, though all they were
entitled to was approximately eight pence, each of them got a

[13] 'Pound' is a better modern equivalent for the word 'denar' than the
AV's 'penny'.
[14] 'Pay the last first.' Why? By this device the first-comers are made to
witness the generous payment of the last, a point necessary to the
development of the story. E. Linnemann, *Parables of Jesus*, 10.

pound in his hand – the full day's wage. But looking on were the first-comers who had begun work at the break of day; and when they noted what the late-comers got, and then themselves received exactly the same amount, the trouble broke. 'These lay-abouts,' they protested, 'have worked only one hour, and yet you have put them on the same level as us who have worked twelve and sweated it out in the noon-day sun. Is this what you call justice?' (It is just the kind of protest any good trade-unionist would make today.) 'Look, my friend,' said the Employer to the chief protester, 'I'm not cheating you. Didn't we agree on a pound a day? Well, you've got it. Be off with you. If it is my pleasure to pay the last the same as you, am I not free to do as I will with what is my own? Or are you jealous because I am kind?'

Why did Jesus tell the story? Was he really discussing the problem of 'the just wage', or indeed any question of economics at all?

To interpret the story rightly, forget the saying, 'So the last will be first and the first last' (Matt. 20.16),[15] and remember two things. First, as we hinted earlier, Jesus was answering his critics the Pharisees, those 'goody-goody' Jews who imagined their piety entitled them to a special claim on God's reward and complained that Jesus was opening the gates of God's kingdom to all the undesirable characters in Israel. Second: the crux of the story comes with that settlement after sunset and the astonishing generosity of the Employer to the late-comers, who assuredly stand for the publicans and sinners. For this is not really the parable of the Labourers in the Vineyard. Not they but the Good Employer is the chief character in it, and the Good Employer represents God.

In short, Jesus is not talking about equal pay for equal work. He is talking not economics but theology. 'The rewards of the kingdom of God,' he is saying, 'are not measured by men's deserts but by their needs. God treats sinners as the good Employer treated those unemployed men. This is what the Almighty is like, and, because he is like this, and acts like this, so do I.'

The man who told this tale knew God's nature and will better than any other born of woman, and what he tells us is as true

[15] See note at the end.

in 1970 as it was in AD 30: 'God is like that Good Employer.
He makes no distinctions among his children. He has no step-
bairns. In an earthly family a good father gives according to his
children's needs and not according to their abilities or deserts.
So it is in that great kingdom over which God rules as Father.'

But, somebody is sure to object, the story is long out-of-date
because the Pharisees are long dead and buried. Are they really?
Does not every age throw up people like them? Have we forgotten how many pious and conventional Christians criticized
and condemned John Wesley for taking the gospel to the
'sinners' of his day – the colliers, weavers, and day-labourers
whom he won for Christ? Have we forgotten how the conventional and well-to-do Christians sneered at William Booth for
offering 'soup, soap and salvation' to the East-enders of London?
Does not every century produce its unlovely crop of self-
righteous Christians who would make a 'closed shop' of God's
kingdom, and try to keep out all who do not measure up to
their standards – yes, keep them out when God is willing to
receive them? Nay, do not there still survive people in our
churches who suppose their piety gives them a special claim
on God's favour and look with loveless eyes on our modern
publicans and sinners?

The parable of the Good Employer – for so it must be re-named
– makes certain things quite clear.

It reminds us, for one thing, how fortunate it is for us all
that God does not deal with us on the basis of strict justice.
Portia in the play had the root of the Christian matter in her
when she told Shylock the Jew:

> Though justice be thy plea, consider this,
> That in the course of justice none of us
> Should see salvation. We do pray for mercy.

Again, it declares that God's thoughts are not our thoughts,
nor his ways our ways, for:

> The love of God is broader than the measure of man's mind.

And it tells us that there is an *equal reward* for all in God's
kingdom. Does this shock and startle us? An equal reward for
even the poorest and least worthy of Christ's followers along

with Paul and Augustine, with Francis and Luther, with Wesley and Livingstone, with William Booth and Dietrich Bonhoeffer? It doesn't make sense, and it doesn't sound fair, but it is the will of God and it is certainly wonderful. This, says Jesus, is what God is like. If he is like this, how dare we be jealous? On the contrary, is not Christ calling us in this parable (as he put it in his great Sermon) to be 'all goodness as our heavenly Father is all good' (Matt 5.48)?

NOTE

There are two good reasons why we should ignore Matt. 20.16 (cf. Matt. 19.30) when interpreting the parable. (1) The parable does not teach the reversal of rank at the end, since all the workers receive the same wage. (2) The saying occurs also in Mark 10.31 and Luke 13.30, i.e. originally it must have been an independent saying of Jesus. Possibly Matt. 20.8 led the evangelist to put it where it now stands. In other words, it is only its context in Matthew which suggests it was first addressed to the disciples.

6

The Men of the Kingdom

Eight parables – the Tower Builder and the Warring King, the Hid Treasure and the Precious Pearl, the Disobliging Neighbour and the Callous Judge, the Farmer and his Man, and the Two Builders – set forth what is required of the men of the kingdom – the readiness to 'count the cost' and sacrifice all for God's cause, the victorious faith and the obedient service to which they are summoned, and the paramount importance of not only hearing Christ's teaching but doing it.

Tower Builder and Warring King (Luke 14.28-33)

I   We like to think of Jesus as the one who cried 'Come'. We need to be reminded that he could also cry 'Count'.

The theme of these twin parables is the cost of discipleship. They seem to come straight out of the time in his Galilean ministry when enthusiasm was running high and not a few were in the mood of the man who said, 'Lord, I will follow you wherever you go' (Luke 9.57).[1] But Jesus 'who could tell what was in a man', who knew how men who make the most glowing promises of fidelity so often fail to finish the course, did not at once say, 'Splendid! Come, join my band of disciples.' Instead, in two stories, he bade the man – and all like him – consider in cold blood all that following him might mean.

The first story was about a farmer who planned to build a tower which would provide shelter for his workers and enable

[1] In Luke's gospel they occur in the record of the long final journey to Jerusalem which begins at Luke 9.31 and in a context whose subject is renunciation.

him to keep watch over his fields. Without stopping to consider whether he had the necessary materials, he rushed ahead with the job, only to find when he had half done, that he had run out of bricks and his money bags were empty. And there, standing gaunt and ludicrous against the sky, was the half-finished tower, a standing monument to his thoughtless folly, so that ever after his neighbours would say as he passed, 'There goes the man who started to build but could not finish!'

The other story was about a king who went to war with a neighbouring monarch. We may suppose he coveted a bit of his realm. So he mobilized his little army in a hurry and sallied forth to take it. But he had scarcely crossed his own frontier when on the horizon he descried his enemy's army. And what an army! On any reckoning it was twice the size of his own. Too late he realized that the battle to be fought could have only one issue, and soon he was sending envoys to ask for terms of surrender.

Those would-be followers of Jesus in Galilee cannot have missed the point. 'You want to follow me?' says Jesus, 'Then first sit down, cast up the balance, and make a sober estimate of the cost'.

This is the other face – the stern face – of the Christ who said to others, 'Come to me, all you who are heavy laden and I will give you rest' (Matt. 11.28). He does not wish to scare away intending followers, but he will have none under false pretences in a campaign which may end in a cross. Not for him the jaunty disciple fired by an impulsive enthusiasm, but only the man who has reckoned with the hard future in prospect and knows that, in spite of all, he has the will and ability to endure. In modern terms, Christ wants no half-way Christians.

II If these two parables apply today, as they do, to the individual life, they teach that Christian discipleship must still be a costing thing, and that the true blessedness of the Christian life can only be experienced by complete commitment to Christ.

One of the Christian classics of our time has the title *The Cost of Discipleship*. It is written by Dietrich Bonhoeffer, and its theme is the costing-ness, in obedience and self-sacrifice, of what it means to be a Christian. None had a better title to speak of this, because in April 1945 Bonhoeffer was executed by Hitler's Black Guards for his loyalty to Christ and his hatred of the devilries of the Third Reich.

Mercifully it falls to few of us to seal our testimony to Christ with our life's blood, as he did. Yet if we would be true Christians, we must be clear what risks, what costs, what burdens it involves.

The risk of faith, to begin with. As faith is 'betting your life there is a God', so Christian faith is 'the grand venture in which we commit our whole soul and future to the confidence that Christ is not an illusion but the reality of God'.[2]

Add to the risk of faith the cost of giving – giving not merely of our money but of ourselves in active personal service, as members of Christ's great working body in the world, which is the church.

And of course there are the endless burdens from which the mere worldling is delivered – the burdens of caring for those who have fallen by the way in life's race, as well as for the hungry, the oppressed and the under-privileged folk in the world.

But the full tale of the risks, the costs, the burdens Christ imposes can never be told. We only know, as Baron von Hügel said, that 'Christianity taught us to care, caring is the greatest thing, caring matters most', and that we must go on caring for others because God has cared for us in Christ. *Noblesse oblige.*

III   In these two parables Christ makes it clear that he will not issue a lying prospectus. He comes bidding each of us count the costs of discipleship. Not a word has he to say about the blessings of following him. Yet there are beatitudes as well as burdens in the Good News he brings – high privileges and promises as well as stern cautions and challenges.

'Come to me,' says Christ, 'and I will make you citizens in that Kingdom over which Abba Father rules as King.' And if we will, he will teach us to see our own little purposes against a yet mightier purpose and ourselves as under-labourers in the service of 'the Love which moves the sun and the other stars'.

'Come to me,' he says again, 'and I will give you a pattern for living – living as God's children should in his world.' That pattern he has sketched for us in his Sermon on the Mount. There we

[2] P. T. Forsyth, *The Person and Place of Jesus Christ*, London 1946, 205.

have his 'guide lines' for the good life – direction, if not direc-
tions. And if we reply that the heights to which he summons us
are too high, are we not also promised the power to help us try
to attain them? For 'the living Christ still has two hands, one to
point the way, the other held out to help us along'.[3]

The final promise is that which the living Lord made through
his servant John the Seer of Patmos, 'Be thou faithful unto
death, and I will give thee the crown of life' (Rev. 2.10).

Thus Christ warns of the costs and names the blessings. 'You
are a free man,' he says to each of us, 'Count the cost. Life is
before you; choose whom you will serve. I offer you a cross; I
offer you also a crown. I offer you struggle; but there will also
be victory. Look life in the face; look death in the face. Sum it
all up, and make your decision.'

Treasure Trove and Precious Pearl (Matt. 13.44f.)

I   In the Spring of 1947 when two Bedouin lads were shepherd-
ing their sheep and goats at Qumran, by the north-western cliffs
of the Dead Sea, an animal went amissing. One of the lads,
searching for it, threw a stone into a small cave in the rock face.
When he heard what sounded like breaking crockery, he took
sudden fright. Later, however, the two lads crept together into
the cave, and there on its floor, stuffed in elongated jars, behold,
roll upon roll of crumbling leather. They had made one of the
biggest archaeological discoveries of modern times. They had
found the first of the now famous Dead Sea scrolls.

One day, some miles north in Galilee, nineteen centuries before, Jesus, proclaiming the glad, good news of God's dawning
kingdom, told a not dissimilar story about the chance discovery
of treasure trove. A farmer was ploughing a field when suddenly
the coulter laid bare a *cache* of precious coins which, years
before, someone had hid to preserve it from advancing armies or
marauding robbers. Making sure no one had seen him, he
shovelled back the earth on the treasure and hurried home to
scrape up every penny to buy the field. (The morality of the
finder's behaviour is not in question. In Jewish law the finder
of money was the keeper.)

[3] T. W. Manson, *Ethics and the Gospel*, London 1960, 68.

On another occasion he told a story about a trader whose business was the search for fine pearls. One day he had news of the sort of pearl he had been seeking for years – a pearl *par excellence*, a pearl nonpareil. Without more ado he sold all his savings and purchased that wonderful pearl.

The parables read like twins, and the point of both is the same: 'How precious is a place in God's kingdom! Is not such blessedness worth any sacrifice?'

But note one difference which may well be significant. In the Hid Treasure the man's wealth comes to him quite unexpectedly – like winning a Premium Bond – whereas in the Precious Pearl he finds it only after long questing. Is not this Jesus' way of suggesting that it is often by very different roads that men come to God's kingdom? Think, for instance, of Matthew the tax-collector of Capernaum. 'Engaged on the business of foreign governments – thinking no more of an Israelite Messiah but only of Egyptian finance and the like – suddenly the Messiah, passing by, says, "Follow me!"; and he rises up, gives him his hand, "Yea to the death"; and absconds from his desk in that electric manner, leaving his cash-box unlocked, and his books for whoso list to balance.'[4] Is not Matthew like the man who found the hidden treasure? Very different it was to be for the man Paul. His road began in distant Tarsus, wound round the school of Rabbi Gamaliel in Jerusalem and ended – only to begin miraculously again – on a desert track outside Damascus ...

There were many ways then – there are many ways still – into the kingdom of God.

II   Come down two or three centuries to the early church, now with written gospels before them and scholars busily interpreting them. To our surprise we find them identifying the Pearl and the Treasure not with the kingdom of God but with Christ himself. (So, for example, Irenaeus: 'The treasure is Christ.') Yet when you stop to think of it, they were not wrong. For you cannot read the gospels percipiently without realizing that to follow Christ is to be *in* the kingdom, that it is where he is, that in fact he embodies the kingdom of God. 'In the gospel,' wrote Marcion, 'the kingdom of God is Christ himself.' And eighteen

[4] J. Ruskin, *St Mark's Rest*, 174.

centuries later Karl Barth[5] declares, 'Jesus spoke of the kingdom of God, and he *was* the kingdom of God'. This is why, after the Resurrection, the apostles preached Christ rather than the kingdom. The gospel of the kingdom was Christ in essence, Christ was the gospel of the kingdom in power. He was the truth of his own greatest gospel. It is wherever he is, and to have him is to ensure it, to possess eternal life.

For proof you need look no further than the third chapter of Philippians. There Paul tells how, like the trader in the tale, he surrendered everything he held dear – all his proud privileges as a Jew – in order to gain the pearl of the kingdom which was Christ, the Christ in whom, as he said, were 'unfathomable riches' (Eph. 3.8), in whom 'were hidden all God's treasures of wisdom and knowledge' (Col. 3.2).

III Come now to the twentieth century and ourselves. Our world contains many religions, with doubtless some grain of God's truth in most of them, since in all generations 'God has not left himself without some witness – some clue to his nature' (Acts 14.13 NEB). But when the chips are really down – when it isn't an armchair argument or a matter for a debating society – but a faith to live by and a person to follow in this queer, riddling world, what else is there – who else is there – but that Christ in whom the apostles and countless Christians down the centuries have found God's Hidden Treasure and Precious Pearl embodied in a Man?

Here in Christ incarnate, crucified, risen, exalted, and now through the Holy Spirit, present with his people, is all that the religious heart of man could desire – the assurance, through the Cross, of God's forgiveness for sinners, the promise and power of new beginning for all who have failed, and a kingdom of God which calls us to service among our fellows and which is invincible and eternal.

Is not this the spiritual 'wealth that demonetizes all other currencies'? Is not this the *summum bonum* for which one might forfeit all the glittering prizes of the world? So said P. T. Forsyth[6]

---

[5] *Table Talk*, Edinburgh 1963, 47.
[6] *The Person and Place of Jesus Christ*, 55.

in his great book on Christ:

I should count a life well spent and the world well lost if, after tasting all its experiences and facing all its problems, I had no more to show at its close, or carry with me to another life, than the acquisition of a real, sure, humble, and grateful faith in the eternal and incarnate Son of God.

And to all forwandered men in our modern world who have lost their spiritual bearings Christ still comes, offering them the Hid Treasure and the Precious Pearl which carry with them the promise and potency of eternal life. Still, as in Galilee, to each and everyone comes the challenge: 'Is not such blessedness worth any sacrifice? Come, follow me, and I will make you possessors of it.'

Disobliging Neighbour and Callous Judge (Luke 11.5-8; 18.2-8a)[7]

Jesus had an unforgettable way of arguing from the human to the divine. For him, God was holy, but he was not, as some modern theologians have held, 'wholly other'. He believed earthly and human analogies could figure forth to men God's nature and will. Human experience was for him a kind of springboard for the adventure of faith. He had a way of saying, 'Take the very best you know among humans. God is all that – and incomparably more.' So, starting from human values, he invited his disciples to project them into the unseen world and find in them a reflection of the invisible God, maker of heaven and earth.

Recall his illustration of 'the asking son':

Is there a man among you who will offer his son a stone when he asks for bread, or a snake when he asks for fish? If you then, bad as you are, know how to give your children what is good for them, how much more will your heavenly Father give good things to those who ask him? (Matt. 2.9-11)

So Jesus encouraged his men to believe in God's goodness. Now as theology is 'faith thinking', so prayer is faith in action. Jesus never defined prayer; he did better – he gave his disciples a pattern prayer, and in his parables bade them 'expect great things from God'.

Take this story about the Disobliging Neighbour (traditionally

---

[7] Luke 18.8b is secondary. See *Interpreting the Parables*, London 1960, 69.

known as the Friend at Midnight). Late one night a hungry friend turned up unexpectedly at a friend's house and caught him without a scrap of bread in his cupboard. (It is the emergencies of life which drive unwilling men to prayer.) The only thing the householder could do was to knock up a neighbour and ask him for three loaves – the usual meal for one person. And very politely (note the 'Friend' of his address) he did, explaining why he had to.

Now peep into the single-roomed house of the sleeping neighbour. His children are bedded in a row on a raised mat, with the parents one at each end, when suddenly at midnight there comes a hammering on the door. The head of the house, startled from his slumbers, is not amused. 'Don't be a confounded nuisance,' he growls to the knocker outside. 'My door was locked long ago. If I get up, I'll disturb the whole family. No, I'm staying where I am – in bed.'

But our hero outside in the dark refuses to take No for an answer. He keeps on knocking till at last in sheer exasperation the neighbour gets up, unbolts the door, and gives him his three loaves.

Jesus is talking to his disciples about prayer, and his argument is 'by contraries' – the point lies not in the similarity but in the contrast. 'If a human friend, however unwilling,' he says, 'can be induced to get up and give help, how much more will God your Father – and Perfect Friend – be ready to supply your needs.'

This is what believing prayer is like. The disciple with a faith like this will open his heart with utter freeness to the unseen Heavenly Father, sure that he will hear him. He will also be able to accept whatever God sends, believing that the All-wise and All-loving God knows his children's needs better than they know themselves.

Seven chapters later in Luke's gospel we find a companion parable to this one. Tradition has named it the Importunate Widow, but it would be better called the Callous Judge.

This time the scene is a law-court, with the plaintiff a poor widow whose opponent has refused to settle a lawful debt. So she keeps coming before the judge and crying, 'Give me justice against my oppressor'. But the judge is, by his own avowal, a man who is swayed neither by religious principle nor by public opinion. At first he does absolutely nothing. A helpless widow, he thinks, without money or influence – why bother about her? (Doubtless when she started up in court, he said 'Next case, please'.) But if the judge could keep on, so could the widow. Next day she was back again bothering him, and this went on day after day till, at last, he relented and gave her justice. 'Maybe I don't give a damn for God or man,' he reasoned, 'yet just because this tiresome woman keeps pestering me and getting on my nerves, I will give her justice.' And he did.

The judge is not offered as a picture of what God is like. Again our Lord's teaching is 'by contraries'. He is not describing God as some dourly ungracious deity who needs to be badgered into compliance. His meaning is: If even this callous judge could be moved to act by the widow's persistence, how much more will God answer his people's prayers for vindication!

What these stories show, as indeed his whole life shows, is how constantly Jesus leaned on God, believing in the power of prayer, believing because he knew the kind of Being the hearer of prayer was – and is. And is not Jesus still calling his followers today to the same kind of prayer?

'Prayer,' said P. T. Forsyth, 'is for the religious life what original research is for science – by it we get contact with reality.' And in one of his books on prayer he wrote: 'I saw in a friend's house a picture by Dürer, the great German painter. Just two tense hands, palms together, and lifted in prayer. I wish I could stamp the picture on the page of this book, and fit it to John Milton's great line – "The great two-handed engine at our door".'

Why in these dark and troubled times don't we Christians make more use of that 'great two-handed engine'? It was Abraham Lincoln who confessed, 'I have been driven many times to my knees by the overwhelming conviction that I had nowhere else to go. My own wisdom and that of all about me seemed insufficient for the day.' It was Lord Tennyson who wrote:

More things are wrought by prayer than this world dreams of.

And a greater than Lincoln or Tennyson who assured his disciples, as he still assures us:

Ask, and it will be given you,
Seek, and you will find,
Knock, and it will be opened to you. (Matt. 7.7)

So, keep knocking!

NOTE

The last four Greek words in Luke 18.7 are difficult. We have followed the rendering of the Jerusalem Bible: 'even when he delays to help them'.

Why does God 'delay' to help his people? Not on the evidence of these two parables, because he is reluctant to give. Nor again because we are meant to bombard the unseen with a barrage of words – 'We are not heard,' said Jesus, 'for our much speaking.' Rather because he may give us what we really need. If we always got what we asked for from God, the result might be disastrous: 'He gave them their request, but sent leanness to their soul' (Ps. 106.5). Again, there are some gifts we can only use when we want them enough, and God waits till we are ready. 'Delay,' as A. B. Bruce once said, 'may be the result of love taking counsel with wisdom.'

The Farmer and His Man (Luke 17.7-10)

What qualities does Jesus look for in the men of the kingdom? High amongst them stands the will to serve God selflessly, without thought of any reward. His disciples must recognize that first and foremost they are servants of God called to unqualified obedience. They should be able to say (in the memorable monosyllables of the Methodist Covenant): 'I am no longer my own but thine. Put me to what thou wilt.'

This is the point of the dry little story about the Farmer and his Man:

Suppose one of you has a servant ploughing or minding sheep. When he comes back from the fields, will the master say, 'Come along at once and sit down'? Will he not rather say, 'Prepare my supper, fasten your belt, and then wait on me while I have my meal; you can have yours afterwards'? Is he grateful to the servant for carrying out his orders? So with you: when you have carried out all your orders, you should say, 'We are servants, and deserve no credit: we have only done our duty.'

'Servants who deserve no credit.' When Jesus told this story, he was thinking of the Pharisees and their 'merit' theology, their belief that they could, by their 'works', lay up a credit balance in the ledgers of heaven. Jesus says: 'You never find a farmer fussing over a servant who has done a hard day's work and carried out his master's orders. So you, my disciples, must never think you can bring God under obligation to yourselves, or put the Almighty in your debt. Should it please God to give you something, it is the gift of his grace, not a reward for services rendered.'

Tough talking to all reward-seekers! But it is not a denial that God rewards his faithful servants. Our Lord says quite firmly that he does. But (as Bultmann puts it)[8] Jesus promises rewards to those who are obedient without thought of reward (Luke 6.35f.) – to people like those in his parable of the Last Judgment who self-forgetfully befriend and succour all the afflicted and unfortunate.

The parable of the Farmer and his Man therefore warns us against importing into religion that book-keeping mentality which imagines we can run up credit with God by our works. Jesus says it can't be done. So does the Apostle Paul.

But the delusion dies very hard. There still survive among us those who think they can establish a claim on God beyond the line of duty. Something of the Pharisee still lurks in their innermost heart. It is to this hidden Pharisee in the heart that the parable is directed. It tells us that we cannot:

> Make out, and reckon on his ways,
> And bargain for His love, and stand
> Paying a price, at His right hand.

It declares that there is not 'enough' with God. When we have done all, we are still unworthy servants of God. Ultimately, we are driven to cry with Thomas Chalmers, in his great simplicity, 'What could I do if God did not justify the ungodly?' or to make Toplady's lines our own:

> Nothing in my hand I bring,
> Simply to thy Cross I cling.

Christian salvation, we need to remind ourselves, lies not in works of 'merit' but in faith – faith in that Christ whom, though he knew no sin, God made to be sin for us, 'that in him we might be made one with the goodness of God himself' (II Cor. 5.21 NEB).

---

[8] *Theology of the New Testament*, I, London 1952, 14.

The Two Builders (Matt. 7.24-7)

What Jesus takes for granted is always significant. What he takes for granted in the parable of the Two Builders is that our human life will contain an element of storm and trouble: 'In the world you will have tribulation' (John 16.33). This being so, what matters supremely is whether we build the house of our life on rock or on sand.

This is a story from real life. Indeed, Jesus may even have seen with his own eyes a sand-based house begin to shake and shudder when the floods rose and the gales blew before the house went crashing in total collapse. The tale is not only full of Palestinian local colour, but is told with that dramatic power we associate with the supreme master of parable. 'Down came the rain, down swept the spate, heavily blew the winds' till we reach the climax, 'Down it fell with a great crash'.

Sometimes we call it the Two Houses. A better name would be the Two Builders; for it is a contrast between a 'prudent' man who took care to found his house on rock deep-hidden below the dry water-course, and a 'stupid' man who rashly reared his dwelling on the smooth sand of the torrent bed. The outcome was predictable: when the great rains of autumn came and the 'wadi' was turned into a raging river, one house stood firm, the other went down like a house of cards.

The wisdom of founding on rock, the folly of founding on sand, is the point of the parable. The rock-built house stands for hearing *and* doing what Christ says; the sand-built house for hearing it only. And the storm is any time of severe testing in the life of man or nation. In such a crisis the secret of security will be a life built on the teaching and person of Christ.

I 'Hearing *and* doing' is what matters – this is the first thing. One of the saddest words Jesus ever uttered was, 'Why do you call me Lord, Lord, and do not do what I tell you?' (Luke 6.46). So it was even with his first followers in Galilee. Though they were quick to admire and applaud his words, they were soon found wanting when it came to practice. And down nineteen centuries the problem has ever been this ghastly gap between profession and practice.

Happily in modern times there has arisen in the church of Christ a new and welcome stress on what is called 'Christian Action' – the realization that 'faith without works is dead', the conviction that, if our Christian witness to the world is to be effective, it must incarnate itself in action, in deeds of compassion to the poor, the hungry, the disinherited, the oppressed, and all the lost children of God, whether it takes the shape of succouring the 'drop-outs' of our own society, providing food for the starving millions in the world, digging wells for the drought-ridden folk of India, or furnishing medical care for all the victims of disease and war in Africa and elsewhere. And we must all pray and resolve that this clarion call to Christian Action will be heard ever more widely in the years to come.

II But in this parable Jesus is not simply saying what men like Carlyle have said many times, that profession which does not issue in action were better suppressed altogether. He is saying: 'It is a question of my way, which is God's way – or disaster.' Listen: 'Everyone who hears these words *of mine* and acts on them ...' The Carpenter of Nazareth stands before men and tells them that he has laid down principles of action which they will neglect at their peril. Observe what a tremendous personal claim is here being made. Only one who was conscious that his will was synonymous with the divine will could have spoken thus. And what he says is this, 'My way – or disaster'.

Nor is there any alibi for us Christians here. We cannot plead that we do not know what Christ's way is. In his great Sermon (Matt. 5-7) he has spelt it out for us. He has told us what kind of people we ought to be; what kind of worship we ought to render; how we ought to behave in society; what kind of attitude we ought to have to God and money; and how we ought to treat other people. Moreover, as Dr Joad once said, 'Most of us know that Christ's prescription for good living is the right one'. Yes, but the prescriber himself goes significantly further. He says, 'Either you act on my prescription – or you court disaster'.

Is not the present state of the world the best evidence that Christ is right? 'What kind of shape is the world, Daddy?' said one modern son to his father. And the father replied, 'The hell of a shape, son'. What is being assailed today is not merely what Bunyan called Mansoul, but man's civilization. To the danger which has always menaced the individual we must add that which now threatens the whole of humanity, and whose emblem is the mushroom cloud first seen over Hiroshima.

Christ's words are coming true. When men despise the divine gentleness of the Beatitudes, when they esteem grabbing better than giving, when they substitute the rule of the jungle for the Golden Rule, there can only be one outcome – disaster. God is not mocked. Men must abide the consequences of their ungodly actions. This is part of what the New Testament means by 'the wrath of God', and there is evidence enough that it is operative here and now in our world.

This parable, therefore, has an almost sinister relevance for us and for the world in which we are living. And if it speaks to the whole human race, it speaks still more pointedly to us who belong to 'the household of faith', to the church of Christ. What it says to us is, 'Sand or Rock? Are you content merely to be nominal Christians, paying lip-service to Christ and his truth, or are you resolved to shape your whole lives by it?'

If you decide to make the wise choice – to build the house of your life on rock and not on sand – Christ gives you no guarantee that the floods and storms will abate. They may even grow worse. What he does promise is that, even if your world is reeling about you, you have the assurance that your house will stand firm, for it is built on that eternal granite which is God.

'When your feet are on the rock,' said Principal David Cairns, during the last war, 'you can exult even in the whirlpool.' That is a truly Christian saying. For the Christian God – the God of the cross and of the resurrection – has the evil of the world, even such a world as ours, in the hollow of his hand, and the nations which rage so furiously are still in the leash of that redeeming God.

If you and I believe this – and it is the heart of the New Testament gospel – we are called and commanded as Christians to go forth and do Christ's will in the world, knowing not only that we are building on the rock of Christ – on God's eternal granite – but also, as Paul said in the greatest passage he ever wrote, that nothing in the world or out of it can separate us from the love of God revealed in Jesus Christ our Lord (Rom. 8.38f.).

7

The Crisis of the Kingdom

Jesus saw his whole ministry moving inexorably to a climax which would involve judgment for God's chosen people. In parable after parable he sought to alert them to the gravity of the situation, and in the end he was to weep over Jerusalem because she 'knew not God's moment when it came' or 'the things which belonged to her peace'. 'It was,' says Forsyth,[1] 'the agony of an old nation not only dying but damned; and all its vast tragedy transpiring not only within the soul of one Man but (chief horror!) by the solemn choice and awful act of that one Man himself, and He its lover. Think of a whole nation proud, stubborn and passionate, with an ingrained belief in a world prerogative and mission, expiring in one Man, in whom also by a dreadful collision was rising the Kingdom of God they had forsworn.'

In the six parables we have chosen – the Way to Court, the Great Supper, the Talents, the Unjust Steward, the Ten Bridesmaids and the Owner's Son – we hear Jesus urging his countrymen to 'discern the signs of the times' and, if it may be, repent. He warns his hearers that they are in grave peril of refusing God's invitation into his kingdom; he pillories Israel's leaders for their unfaithful stewardship of God's revelation entrusted to them; he tells them that they must act with resolution and not be caught unprepared. And in his final parable he predicts the doom that awaits them if they reject God's last appeal to his people in the person and mission of his Messiah.

[1] *The Expositor*, July 1915.

The Way to Court (Luke 12.57-9; cf. Matt. 5.25f.)[2]

I   Jesus was far more interested in politics – the politics of his own nation in relation to God's eternal purpose – than many pious Christians have supposed. One of the many gospel evidences in proof of this is the parable of the Way to Court, or, as it is often called, the Defendant. It concludes a passage (Luke 12.35-9) heavy with Jesus' foreboding about the crisis which overhung Israel. Read it again, and you will see that the parable is the last of five (the others are the Waiting Servants, the Sleeping Householder, the Man in Charge, and the Weather Signs) in which Jesus foresees the coming crisis and calls on his countrymen to read the signs of the times and act accordingly. 'How weatherwise you can all be,' he says to them, 'O, if only you could be as spiritually wide-awake to what is happening in this nation now!' Then he speaks the parable of the Way to Court:

> While you are going with your opponent (your creditor) to the court, make an effort to settle with him while you are on the way; otherwise he may drag you before the judge, and the judge hand you over to the constable, and the constable put you in jail. I tell you, you will not come out till you have paid the last farthing.

There are four parties in the parable – the insolvent debtor, the creditor, the judge and the constable. How do we interpret it?

The insolvent debtor on the way to court is Israel. The way to court is Jesus' way of describing the impending crisis in his nation's history, a crisis which, he says, will bring testing for his followers, God's judgment on the nation, and a blood baptism for himself. Israel stands at the cross-roads, and she must decide which way she will go. She must choose whether to align herself with God's purpose embodied in himself and his ministry or, refusing and pursuing the path of nationalism, enter on a collision course with Rome which must end in her ruin. What makes the decision so urgent is the shortness of the time. If his countrymen were in similar straits financially, if they were insolvent debtors on the way to court, they would settle with their creditor

---

[2] Matthew has turned the parable into an example story about the need for reconciliation with one's brother. The best discussion of the parable known to me (and to which I am indebted) is G. B. Caird in *The Expository Times* for November 1965.

long before they reached it. But, alas, in the far more momentous crisis of their nation, 'eyes have they but they see not'. Could they but realize their peril, they would see that the only right thing to do was to turn, before it was too late, and come penitently to the living God whose great purpose in history goes forward whether men will or no!

Consider the historical situation as Jesus saw it in the light of God's purpose for the world. God has chosen Israel to be his servant – to be the bearer to the world of 'a light to lighten the Gentiles', that they too might come to a knowledge of his saving truth. But Israel, by rejecting God's kingdom and Messiah, was repudiating her part in God's great plan. Was the divine purpose to be stultified and frustrated by Israel's disobedience? No, in the mission of Jesus God the great sower had sown the seed and it would yet yield a bountiful harvest. But the certainty of God's ultimate victory did not absolve Israel from the need to choose. And now the sands were fast running out ... Like the debtor in the tale, Israel had her one last chance to escape the toils of the law and the judge's sentence.

Such was the original meaning of the parable.

II The historical crisis which produced it is long past. It came to a head in the whole complex of events which began with Jesus' ministry and culminated, a generation later, in Israel's fatal clash with Rome. Visit Masada today, and you will see where the Jews made their last heroic stand. But if old Israel, by her disobedience, forfeited her place in God's purpose, that purpose was not thwarted. For out of that crisis was born the new Israel, which is the church of Christ.

Yet, though the crisis now lies in 'the dark backward and abysm of time', this does not mean that Jesus' parable has nothing to say to us today.

In every age crises of one sort or another confront the church. One came in the sixteenth century with the Reformation. A very different one faced the faithful in the nineteenth with the coming of Darwinism and the doctrine of evolution. Today South Africa's policy of *Apartheid* constitutes yet another crisis for the church and the world. And so on.

With the help of hindsight, it is very easy for us to condemn

Israel's blindness in her crisis nineteen hundred years ago. But
has the new Israel never been blind to the signs of the times
and failed to interpret aright God's action in history? Think
back to the years just before 1914. When the crisis of the
Great War broke on the world, were there not many calling
themselves Christians who found their faith sadly unsettled by
that catastrophe? How could there be a good God, they said, if
he permitted such horror and suffering to happen? If they had
interpreted the times with truly Christian eyes, as prophets like
P. T. Forsyth[3] did, how very differently they might have con-
strued the catastrophe! They might have seen that, with such a
Europe, with such a neglect of God and his righteousness, the
wonder, the disquieting thing would have been if no divine
judgment had fallen on our materialistic civilization and our
degenerate Christianity. How degenerate it was, Albert Schweitzer[4] bore witness. Writing home from Lambarene in Christmas
1914 he said:

We are, all of us, conscious that many natives are puzzling over the
question how it can be possible that the whites, who brought them the
Gospel of Love, are now murdering each other, and throwing to the
winds the commands of the Lord Jesus. When they put the question to
us, we are helpless.

Indeed, dare we say today – even after a Second World War –
that we have learnt the lessons God teaches us in the crises of
history and interpreted them in the light of his nature and
purpose disclosed in Christ?

It is a question worth the most serious pondering; for since
our scientists have learnt how to split the atom, the issues for
mankind have grown immeasurably graver. If we view things
in the perspective of eternity, may we not see in the invention
of the atomic bomb God's awful warning to modern man of his
potential to destroy himself and his world? Is not our so-called
Christian civilization now in the position of the debtor in Christ's
parable? If we persist in the politics of blatant self-interest and
'devil take the hindmost', if we fail to heal the open sores of
humanity – racialism, world-hunger and the rest – if we do not
resolutely attack the problems which cause nation to strive

[3] In his book *The Justification of God* (1917).
[4] *On the Edge of the Primeval Forest*, London 1922, 138.

against nation, and if our statesmen do not come together and for ever ban the making and stock-piling of atomic missiles, will not our civilization, sooner or later, be in peril of 'paying the last farthing' in nuclear holocaust?

This is surely the biggest crisis which now faces the world, and the church, in its prophetic role, ought to be facing men with the dread issues, saying to this generation, as Christ said to his, 'You know how to interpret the appearance of earth and sky; but why do you not know how to interpret the present time?'

'He who has ears to hear, let him hear.'

The Great Supper (Luke 14.15-24)[5]

When the Jews of Jesus' day dreamt of the time when God would finally set up his kingdom, they often pictured it as a great supper or banquet. It was thus the pious man was thinking when, sitting one day at table with Jesus, he observed, 'How happy will the man be who sits down to feast in the Kingdom of God!' Such a remark could only have come from one who was tolerably sure of his own invitation to God's banquet. The story with which Jesus answered him must have shocked him out of his own complacency.

It was about a host who prepared a great supper to which he had previously invited guests. When the banquet day dawned, and 'all things were ready', he sent 'a servant' (a veiled reference to Jesus' own mission) to remind the guests that the day had arrived. (This double bidding accords with Eastern custom.) But at the crucial moment the invited guests suddenly found they had more important things to do – property to be inspected, oxen to be tested before buying, a new wife to be cosseted and cared for – and they all at once made excuses for absence.

Predictably, the host was 'not amused'. Determined to fill all the places at his table, he now sent his servant on a new search, first for the waifs in the streets and alleys (which must mean the publicans and sinners) and then, when there was still room, for the vagrants in the highways and hedges (which suggests

[5] On the parallel parable in Matthew of The Marriage Feast, see *Interpreting the Parables*, 55f.

the Gentiles). 'Constrain them to come in,' he told his servant, 'for I want my house to be full.' (This is a hint at the universal inclusiveness of God's kingdom.) 'For,' said the host conclusively, 'those originally invited have forfeited their claim to places at my table.'

So the parable of the Great Supper might be re-named the story of 'the Contemptuous Guests'.

What Jesus was saying to his pious friend was something like this: 'You think that God's kingdom is a future prospect to be contemplated with unctuous sentiments. You are wrong. It is a present and pressing reality, and it is calling for your immediate response.

'Long ago God called Israel to be the people of God, and now, at his accepted time, he has renewed his invitation to share in his kingdom, only to see it deliberately neglected and rejected by his own people. So now God opens the doors of his kingdom to all the despised and lost children of God.'

Jesus spoke his parable to the churchmen in Israel, the professedly religious in the land. But the story has not lost its relevance for us.

Through the cross and the resurrection and by the gift of the Holy Spirit at Pentecost, the kingdom of God was thrown open to all men with faith. But, as in the parable the invited guests, finding more important things to do, were quick to reply, 'Please make my excuses for absence', so men still do, and basically their excuses are the same.

'I am in the act of buying an estate,' said the first man, 'and I must inspect it before purchase.' For 'estate' write 'investments' and you have the modern man's equivalent. How many are so preoccupied with increasing their material possessions that they have no time to hear the call, 'Be still and know that I am God' – the God who is calling them now into his kingdom which is man's highest blessedness. In Shaw's *Saint Joan* there is a conversation between the Maid and the Dauphin. Joan heard voices from God telling her what to do. The Dauphin was exasperated. 'Oh, your voices, your voices,' he said, 'Why don't the voices come to me? I am King, not you.' And the Maid answered, 'They do come, but you don't hear them.' Many of us today are like the Dauphin. 'The world is too much with us; late and soon' for us ever to hear and obey the call of God.

'I am in the act of buying five yoke of oxen,' said the second refuser, 'and I must try them out before I buy.' Nowadays I suspect the same man's excuse would be in terms not of five yoke of oxen but of 'ten iron horses' – of a motor car which is the image many a modern man worships. How often are our churches half-empty on a Sunday morning? What are the people doing whose fathers and forefathers would have been found in their pews on the Lord's Day? They are polishing their Minis or their Mercedes; they are bowing down before the metallic idols of our time. So easy it is for a new brazen image made by human hands to engross a man's waking thoughts and actions that he can find no space for God in his life.

'I have just married a wife,' said the third man in the story, 'and therefore I cannot come.' The 'wife' stands for the new happiness of married life and a home of one's own. Now beyond any doubt these are among the finest of the earthly blessings which the good God gives us

> To make a happy fire-side clime
> To weans and wife,
> That's the true pathos and sublime
> Of human life.

But it is one of the tragedies of life when good things like these are allowed to shut out the claims of God.

Worldly possessions, business preoccupations, domestic ties, are still the things which make men deaf to the claims of God's kingdom. So easy it is for a man to become absorbed in the things of time that he forgets the things of eternity. We can be so busy making a livelihood that we have no time to make a life.

There is a Danish fable which tells how a spider once slid down a filament of thread from the rafters of a lofty barn and established himself on a lower level. There he spread his web, caught plenty of flies, and grew sleek and prosperous. One day, wandering about his premises, he saw the thread which stretched up into the unseen above him. 'What is that for?' said the spider, and snapped it. And all his little house of life collapsed about him.

The point of the fable is surely plain.

From the three excuse-makers come back again now to the

main story. One point clearly made in it is that nobody is excluded from God's kingdom except by his own choice. Christ here gives no support to any doctrine of 'double predestination' or a God who sends one to heaven and ten to hell all for his glory.

But we totally misunderstand the parable if we do not hear urgently sounding through it, 'Now is the accepted time!' The pious man said, 'How happy will he be who sits down hereafter at the banquet in God's kingdom!' Jesus' reply was: 'If a man does not accept God's invitation to his banquet now, it will be too late.'

God's invitation, through Christ, into his kingdom is always going out; and we are all even now writing our answers. Either it is, 'Please make my apologies', which is only another way of saying 'I have more important things to do'. Or else it is, 'I know my heart's need. I am weary of my sins and need forgiveness. O God, you have offered me it in Christ, and with all my heart I accept it.'

As Jesus himself said in his first Beatitude, 'How blest are those who know their need of God!' (Matt. 5.3 NEB).

The Talents (Matt. 25.14-26)

When you and I speak of a 'talent', we use the word as Milton did in the famous sonnet on his blindness:

> And that one talent which is death to hide,
> Lodg'd with me useless ...

'Talent' means a natural gift, in Milton's case a gift for writing sublime poetry. But in New Testament times a 'talent' was a unit of coinage and meant a lot of money. In present-day values it must have been worth at least £5,000. We have to think, then, of the first servant in the story being given £25,000, the second £10,000, and the third £5,000. But the precise amounts do not matter, for the story is about faithfulness rather than finance, and it might well be renamed 'Money in Trust'.[6]

Recall the outline of the story. A rich man, about to go

[6] C. H. Dodd's title for it. On Luke's parallel parable of the Pounds, see *Interpreting the Parables*, 79f.

abroad, entrusted his servants with the sums already mentioned, expecting them to put the monies to good use in his absence. When he returned from his travels, he called them to account for their stewardship. Two of the servants had greatly increased their capital, and received splendid promotion as well as their master's 'Well done'. But the third confessed that, fearing to risk his master's money, he had buried it for safety in the ground. He now restored to his master the exact sum he had received. But if he expected praise from his master, he was rudely undeceived. 'You lazy scoundrel,' said the master, 'you put me down, didn't you, for a man who drives a hard bargain. You ought to have invested the money in the bank, and I would have got it back now with interest.' So 'the lazy scoundrel' was relieved of the £5,000 which was then given to his more enterprising colleague.

What is the point of this parable? That we all have a varying endowment of talents (natural gifts), and that if we don't use them, we lose them? That is true enough, but it was not our Lord's original meaning. All Jesus' parables, in one way or another, bore on a definite historical situation – the coming of God's kingdom in his ministry – and they were usually aimed at particular groups of his contemporaries. Remember also that Jesus saw his ministry as the supreme crisis in God's dealings with Israel, and that this story of the Money in Trust is one of several parables in which he warned Israel and her leaders of the divine judgment overhanging them.

The other thing to note is that our parable has three characters, and that by the 'rule of end stress' the spotlight falls on the third one – in this case, the 'lazy scoundrel' who had done nothing with the money entrusted to him. For whom does he stand? He stands for the religious leaders of Israel. God had entrusted them with his Word – his unique revelation of himself and his will in the Law and Prophets – and they had 'fallen down' on their trust. They had hoarded away that saving knowledge of God which should have been 'a light to lighten the Gentiles and the glory of his people Israel'. They had kept for themselves what was meant for mankind. Such hoarding was tantamount to defrauding God of his own, and for this they would have to answer. As in fact they did.

How then does the parable apply to Christians today? The answer is not in doubt. The church now stands where the old Israel once stood, faced by the same Lord, confronted by the same divine demands. 'Trade till I come,' is still his command, and the question which he puts to us is this, 'What have you done with the spiritual wealth I entrusted to you for all men?'

The gospel, Paul tells us, 'is the power of God unto salvation for everyone who has faith' (Rom. 1.15). It is God's dynamic for saving sinful men and women. Have we always been faithful stewards of that spiritual dynamic? Have we proclaimed the gospel in its apostolic fulness and grandeur, or have we watered it down to meet the mood of the age, so muting its challenge and robbing it of its power? Have we been true heralds of the grace of God to the 'lost' men and women of our time, or have we allowed our preoccupation with our own petty ecclesiastical concerns to block the clear witness which Christians ought to be making to a sin-sick and fear-ridden world?

It is putting the same point in another way if we say that the parable is a rebuke to all 'safety first' Christians among us. Dr David Read[7] tells us of a fellow captive in a German POW camp in the last war. Like the rest of the prisoners, he regularly received blocks of chocolate in parcels from home. And for the last three months of the war he stored away every slab of chocolate, wrapping it in paper and cardboard. Suddenly came the order to move and jettison all baggage. Off went the man to secure his precious chocolate, only to find, when he unwrapped his parcel, a heap of uneatable mould.

There are Christians like this man. They would like to wrap up their religion and keep it close, says Dr Read. They say, 'Better far to preserve our religious heritage than to expose it to new ideas'. Or, 'Better far to see that our own country is kept Christian than indulge in the luxury of Foreign Missions'. So they scurry down the funk-holes of orthodoxy in the name of defending the faith and never expose it to the bigger world where the wind of God's Spirit is blowing bracingly and cathartically.

Jesus' story of the Money in Trust, therefore, says to all such timorous and 'safety first' Christians: 'If you do not use, you

[7] *Expository Times*, September 1951, p.374.

will lose. Trade till I come. If you don't expand and adventure in the Christian emprise, you betray the gospel.' Why? Because only as you 'launch out into the deep', will the kingdom of God become real to you, and be a blessing to the world. And it is only the Christian who is ready to take risks and let the leaven of the gospel do its God-given work among men, who at the end of the day will hear his Master's 'Well done, good and faithful servant! Enter thou into the joy of thy Lord'.

The Unjust Steward (*Luke 16.1-8*)

I   To judge by the discussion it has evoked, this is the most puzzling of all Christ's parables. It is the tale of a rogue's skulduggery when threatened with ruin. And yet, when he told it, Jesus apparently praised the chief character in it for his sharp practice.

Why did Jesus tell the story? The answer is that he used the tale to alert his hearers to energetic and decisive action in a time of crisis – the supreme crisis then impending over Israel.

Let us hear the story again. It goes very nicely and naturally into Scots where 'laird' is the northern form of 'lord', and 'factor' the title of the man who manages the laird's estate. Let us call it the tale of the Rascally Factor.

There was a wealthy laird, said Jesus, who had a dishonest factor. When somebody whispered to the laird that his factor was slowly ruining him – possibly by feathering his own nest out of the estate – the laird summoned him and faced him with his villainy. 'You had better turn in your accounts,' he said, 'for I mean to sack you.'

The factor wasted no time in cursing the laird or those who had 'split' on him. He did a bit of quick thinking. 'I'm going to get my books,' he reflected, 'but what am I to do afterwards? Manual labour is not for me – I'm too soft. And I'm too proud to take to the road and beg. But wait! I think I have it. Even if I am going to lose my job, I can still see a way of keeping in with my friends.'

So he summoned the chief farmers who had loans from the estate. When the first appeared, the factor asked, 'What is your debt to the laird?' 'A thousand gallons of oil.' 'Very well,' said the factor, 'call it five hundred.' To the next farmer he said, 'How much do you owe?' 'A thousand bushels of wheat.' 'Right,' said the factor, 'take your pen and change the figure from a ten to an eight.' And so, by deliberately falsifying the accounts, the factor put the two farmers under a lasting obligation to himself and secured their future friendship and a roof over his head.

Such is the tale, which was probably based on a real-life incident; but the surprise is still to come. For we read that when Jesus had ended the story, 'the Lord' – and this means Jesus, not the laird[8] – commended the dishonest factor because he had acted so shrewdly.

Why did Jesus praise this scoundrel? Not certainly for his roguery and rascality. He praised him for his resource and resolution when he was in a tight corner. For, as Jesus said sadly, 'the sons of this world are in their generation wiser than the sons of light'.

Jesus was speaking to his fellow-countrymen in a time of great crisis. His hearers must have been both surprised and indignant to hear Jesus commend the scoundrelly factor. 'Well for you to be indignant,' said Jesus, 'but you should apply the lesson to yourselves. You are in much the same position as the factor – only that the crisis which now threatens you is far more terrible. The factor, in his personal crisis, sized up the situation shrewdly and acted boldly, with the purpose of securing his own future. For you, too, the challenge of the hour calls for like resolute and decisive action.'

II The unique historical crisis – God's coming to old Israel in blessing and judgment – is now a matter of past history. Does this mean that the parable has nothing to say to us today? On the contrary! It is a truism to say that the church lives today in a time of crises, and Christ is still calling his Christians to show resource and courageous action in face of them.

There are many issues in our day which challenge the church – as they threaten mankind's whole future and well being – and which demand clear thinking and bold action in Christian terms. One is the colour question. Another is the call to church unity in face of our unhappy and damaging divisions. And a third is

[8] See note at end.

the supreme issue of war and peace now become so much more urgent through the risk of nuclear holocaust. Why doesn't the church rise to the challenge of these issues and speak and act with great boldness in Christ's name?

'The sons of this world,' said Jesus, 'are wiser in their generation than the sons of light.' Is this not still true? The modern 'sons of this world' – we call them nowadays 'the secularists' – are all too often found acting with an energy and decision which puts Christ's followers to shame. Thus your ardent Communist, though he has no hope of a Hereafter, will devote all his time and talents to spreading his Marxist propaganda and collaring the key positions in trade-unions, while your average church member seems to find it impossible to devote a little bit of his own expertise or skill to the service of the church in his own community or in the wider world. Cannot we hear Christ, the King and Head of the church, still saying to us through this parable, 'Oh, if only my Christians would bring to the work of God's cause and kingdom one half of the resource and resolution that the sons of this world bring to theirs!'

NOTE
That 'the Lord' (*Ho Kyrios*) means Jesus is proved by three things:
1. The Laird would hardly have praised a man who had nearly ruined him.
2. 'The Lord' (18 times in Luke's gospel) always means Jesus.
3. The analogy of Luke 18.6.
V.9 has nothing to do with the parable. Its point is that by disposing of worldly wealth in a proper way we may have treasure in heaven. The one effective way to deal with 'dirty' money is to free it for the service of God.

The Ten Bridesmaids (Matt. 25.1-12)

Here is a story from first-century Palestine about ten village girls on their way to a wedding, five of whom skimped their preparations and lived to rue their carelessness.

How true to life are its details you may judge from the experience of a modern visitor to Palestine. Dr J. A. Findlay[9] has related how, on nearing the gates of a Galilean town, he saw ten maidens gaily clad and playing a musical instrument as they danced along the road in front of his car. His guide told him

[9] *Jesus and his Parables*, London 1950, 111f.

that the girls were going to keep the bride company till the bridegroom arrived. Was there any chance of seeing the wedding? The guide doubted it: 'It might be tonight or tomorrow night ...' Sometimes, he explained, the bridal party might be caught napping. The bridegroom might come unexpectedly, even in the middle of the night. So the bridal party must always be ready to go out to meet him. No one, he further explained, was allowed in the streets after dark without a lighted lamp; and once the bridegroom had arrived, the door was shut, and late-comers were refused admission.

In the parable the ten girls, friends of the bride, planned to go out and meet the bridegroom when he came with his friends to conduct the bride to his house for the wedding. Their role was to provide a lighted escort for the bridegroom's party. But, as sometimes happens at weddings, there was a hitch. All ten bridesmaids appeared with lighted torches; but only five remembered to bring oil in flasks to replenish them, if the bridegroom should somehow be delayed (e.g. in finalizing some detail of the marriage settlement).

In fact, he was delayed, so that, wearied with waiting, the ten girls dozed off to sleep, and it was midnight before the shout went up, 'The bridegroom's on his way'. It was then that five girls found their torches going out for lack of oil. They tried to borrow from the other five, who had brought extra, only to be told, 'No, there won't be enough for all of us'. A fair enough reply: better five torches all the way than ten only a part of it. So away went the foolish five in search of oil. They were not long gone when the bridegroom did arrive, and the five wise girls went off with him and his friends to the wedding. Later, when the five foolish turned up breathlessly, they found the reception door shut. 'Let us in! Let us in!' they begged. But all they got from the bridegroom was a dusty answer, as though to say, 'If you can't turn up in time, you don't deserve to be here'.

'And the door was shut.' What a grim ending to what should have been a happy-ending story! When did Jesus tell it?

The answer is that this is one of several parables (e.g. Waiting Servants and the Burglar) in which Jesus warned his hearers that the supreme crisis in God's dealings with his chosen people was approaching, that the Messiah was coming to the very heart and home of Jewry, and that the issue for them could only be disaster if, like the foolish girls, they let themselves be caught unprepared.

It is a matter of history that Israel was caught unprepared. When God sent his Messiah among them, the Jews were both unready and unrecipient. As St John said sadly, 'He came to his own home, and his own people did not receive him' (John 1.11). But out of that crisis was born a new Israel, the church of Christ. If that church looked back to the cross and resurrection, it also looked forward to the time when Christ would come in glory; and, naturally enough, they re-applied Christ's story to their own situation,[10] seeking to alert their members for that glorious coming.

Today, like them, we still stand 'between the times', between Christ's First and Second Comings. Christ himself did not know the time of his coming in glory (Mark 13.32). No more do we, and it is foolish to speculate on what is a reserved secret in the breast of God. But this does not lessen the need for Christians to be prepared.

Writing on this matter, Professor Moule[11] has well said:

New Testament thought on the Last Things, at its deepest and best, always concentrates on what God has already done for men in Christ. It does not say, How long will it be before the final whistle blows full time? Rather it says, Where ought I to be to receive the next pass? What really matters is that the kick-off has already taken place, the game is on, and we have a captain to lead us to victory.

'Where ought I to be to receive the next pass?' This is a modern way of expressing the call to preparedness. We know him whom we shall meet when the human race reaches its last frontier post and comes face to face with God in Christ. Christ is both our captain now, who, unseen but not unknown, leads us to victory, and the one who will confront us at God's last great reckoning with men. Then, 'when the books are opened', it will emerge whether, like the wise girls in the story, we have prepared ourselves for it or whether, like the foolish ones, we have neglected to do so.

[10] See Note at end.
[11] *The Birth of the New Testament*, London 1966, 101f.

Our Lord, in the gospels, has taught us how we ought to prepare for the great Day – by steadfast prayer, by daily obedience to God's will, by showing forgiveness to our fellow men, by sacrificial love to all in need.

The question is: Are we preparing now before it is too late? Or have we allowed the lamp of our life to go out?

NOTE

The evidence that the church re-applied the parable to its own situation is threefold:

1. Matthew includes it among his parables relating to the Parousia or Second Coming – see its setting in Matt. 24-5.

2. Matt. 25.1 'Then (*tote*, a favourite word of Matthew's) the kingdom of heaven will be like this' means, 'Then when the Day comes'.

3. The 'generalizing conclusion' in Matt. 25.13 ('Watch therefore') does not fit the story, for *all* the girls, wise as well as foolish, went to sleep. But it does fit the situation of the early church expecting Christ's coming in glory.

The Owner's Son (Mark 12.1-9)

This parable has the distinction of being probably the last one Jesus ever told. The Lord has ridden in meek majesty into the Holy City and cleansed the Temple, thus setting in train the whole series of events destined to issue in the doom of Jerusalem and the rise of the new Israel. Now in the Holy City itself the rulers of Jewry have resolved to make an end of this Messianic pretender; the skies are louring; and calvary is not far away.

It is to these rulers that Jesus tells the story which is half parable, half allegory. Many of its words occur in Isaiah's Song of the Vineyard (Isa. 5.1-7) where the prophet had likened Israel to God's Vineyard which had not yielded its proper fruit and was due for judgment. But if some of the words in Jesus' tale are old, the application is new and startling.

A man, Jesus tells them, planted a vineyard, and when he had set it in order, let it out to some tenants before he went abroad. He made a bargain with them on a crop-sharing basis; at vintage time they were to pay him as rent a share of the produce. Accordingly, when the time came round, he sent one of his servants to collect it. But an absentee landlord is fair game for unscrupulous tenants. They paid the servant – with blows;

a second servant whom he sent they outraged; and a third they slew. And so on.

Desperate situations require daring remedies. The Owner now conceived a bold idea. 'They have treated my servants thus,' he said to himself, 'but if I send my own son they must respect him.' But the tenants were worse than he supposed. When the son appeared, they whispered to each other, 'This is the heir'. 'If we get rid of him, the property will be ours.' So they killed him, cast his body unburied outside the vineyard and seized the vineyard.

'What do you think the Owner of the vineyard will do?' said Jesus as he ended his tale. 'He will come and give the vineyard to others.'

Some have doubted whether Jesus could have so spoken. But there is no reason why Jesus should not have spoken in this allegorical way, provided the symbols used were congruous with both the content of the story and his own actual circumstances.[12]

As indeed they are. In the agrarian discontent of the time, it might have been just a typical story of what befell an absentee landlord's property. But it wasn't. *Gulliver's Travels* is now a young people's classic. But how many of our young people who read it realize that Dean Swift, its author, meant it as a biting comment on his own contemporaries?

So, too, is Jesus' story. For the vineyard is Israel, the people whom God had chosen to be the special recipients of his grace, that they in turn might make it known to the whole world. The tenants are the rulers of Israel down the centuries. The servants are the prophets from Elijah to John the Baptist. And the only son and heir is Christ himself.

The parable, therefore, is our Lord's picture of Israel's history. Thus and thus did God deal with his people and thus and thus have they treated his messengers. 'O Jerusalem, Jerusalem, who killest the prophets,' he said (Luke 13.34). And now events are moving to their awful climax ...

So, after all, it was not a story in which all the characters were fictitious. It was, in fact, autobiography. For the man who told it was its central figure, and within a brief time the tale came fully true. God sent his only son to his people, making

[12] G. V. Jones, *op. cit.*, 90.

his last appeal; and they spiked him to a cross, outside the northern wall of Jerusalem.

It is an old story now; but we cannot simply dismiss it by saying that it is about some first century Jews and therefore no concern of ours. We belong to the new Israel which is the church of Christ; and if the church has inherited Israel's place, it inherits also the danger of God's judgment. Let us consider the point more fully.

The Jews killed the Owner's son, but they did not end his life. They but released it for wider and fuller work. What Caiaphas, Pilate and the others were trying to do on the first Good Friday was to stop the ministry of Jesus. But if there is one thing certain in the record of what followed, it is that the ministry of Jesus *went on*. It goes on still. The Owner's son is no longer 'cribbed, cabined and confined' within the little land of Palestine. Through the Holy Spirit's work, he has become the living Lord of some nine hundred million followers. Moreover, God's vineyard is now co-terminous with the globe itself. Its tenants are no longer the Jews but ourselves and men of practically every race under the sun. And to us in this twentieth century the parable comes with its Word of God for our time.

It speaks, first, in judgment. We are God's tenants. To us, as to old Israel, God looks for the fruits of faith and love and obedience. Of us he requires that we do justly and love mercy and walk humbly with our God. Dare we say that we are producing these fruits?

True, as we look out over the earth, we see today an *ecclesia*, a church, which is in a true sense world-wide. The mustard seed has grown into a great tree in whose branches the wild birds have come to roost. But, alas, there is another and darker side to the picture. Still, as in Christ's day, 'the great ones of the Gentiles' lord it over their weaker brethren. White men oppress their black brothers. Still this earth which is the Lord's and 'might be fair and free', they parcel out as if it were their own. And as our vision passes from America to Europe and Asia, we see how many places in God's vineyard men have turned into armed camps from which they menace each other with guided missiles. With so much devilry abroad in the earth, it is of the Lord's mercy that we are not consumed.

Nor is it hard to hear the parable speaking to us in challenge. 'Having yet therefore one son, his well-beloved, he sent him last.' Christ is God's last appeal, his final challenge to us rebellious men. 'Here in my Son,' says God, 'I have shown you all my heart – revealed my deepest purposes of mercy and love. Will you not turn and heed him and obey?' So when a man faces the question, 'What shall I do with Christ?', it is God himself challenging us to decide for or against him. Let no man, high or humble, treat that challenge lightly.

Finally, the parable speaks to us in hope. 'They will reverence my son.' And, be it soon or be it late, in the end men will. For Christ is the heir of all that God has made and is yet to come into his own. God's purpose is that men shall be 'joint heirs' with Christ, 'the eldest among a large family of brothers' (Rom. 8.29). For the present men may make havoc of God's vineyard, but they will not do so for ever. For, unless Christ and his apostles are liars and the gospel a gigantic fiction, we look for a time when he who now reigns at God's right hand will, openly and triumphantly, come into his full inheritance, and the Lord of the vineyard will hold a final accounting. Happy the man who on that day will be adjudged a faithful tenant in his Master's vineyard!

8

Eternal Issues

Four parables – not easily fitted into the four main categories preceding – we have subsumed under the title 'Eternal Issues' because they deal with the question of salvation, final judgment and eternal life. They are: The Good Samaritan (which answers the lawyer's question about 'eternal life'), Dives and Lazarus (which was probably directed at the Sadducees who did not believe in a future life), the Last Judgment (which answers the question, 'By what criterion will the heathen be judged?') and The Narrow Door (in which Jesus replies to a man who had asked him, 'Are only a few to be saved?').

The Good Samaritan (Luke 10.25-37)

P. G. Wodehouse (we may recall) defined a parable as a Bible story which at first sounds like an interesting yarn but 'keeps something up its sleeve which suddenly pops up and leaves you flat'. There is truth in this. A parable can sometimes be a means of getting a man to drop his guard and so reveal the man to himself. In the Old Testament the best example is the prophet Nathan's story to King David about the little ewe lamb (II Sam. 12) with its final and devastating 'Thou art the man'. In the New Testament the finest example is Christ's story to the 'lawyer' about the Samaritan, with its final and equally devastating 'Go and do thou likewise'.

1 The 'lawyer' in our parable was a scribe or expert in the

Law of Moses with all its many rules and regulations. And the whole encounter between Jesus and this man spotlights, as we shall see, the difference between the ethic of law and the ethic of love.

To understand the exchanges between the lawyer and Jesus, we must remember that, long before this, wise teachers in Israel had summed up the Law of Moses by putting together the two commands of love to God (Deut. 6.5) and love to neighbour (Lev. 19.18). When therefore the lawyer put his 'test' question to Jesus, 'Master, what must I do to inherit eternal life?' it was not because he wished to know the answer but because he wanted to cross-examine Jesus as an interpreter of the sacred Law.

But note how cleverly Jesus turned the tables on his cross-examiner, first by showing that the lawyer already knew the answer to his question, and then by making him measure his own life by the standard he was setting up in this battle of wits.

Here it is necessary to remember that the pious Jews of the time regarded 'neighbour' as a term of limited liability. They could never allow that neighbour in Lev. 19.18 ('You shall love your neighbour as yourself') included Gentiles or heretical Samaritans. Remembering this, we may come back to the lawyer's question, 'What must I do to inherit eternal life?' Jesus did not answer his question at all: he asked another in his reply, 'What has the Law, or your reading of it, to say about the question?' When the lawyer replied, 'You shall love the Lord your God with all your heart, and your neighbour as yourself', Jesus said, 'Quite right. Act like this, and you are on the way to eternal life'. In other words, stop theorizing about love and get down to practising it.

It was then that the lawyer, gravelled by this dusty (and as we should say, 'existential') answer, put the question he was really spoiling to ask, 'And who, pray, is my neighbour? Where am I to draw the line?'

But, to his chagrin, Jesus declined the debate. Seeing it was time to strike home, he told instead a story, not to answer the man's question but to show him that it was the wrong question. The right question is not, 'Whom may I regard as neighbour?'

but 'To whom can I be one?' And the right answer to that question is, 'To anyone whose need serves a claim on my help'.

II First we see the lonely traveller – doubtless a Jew – making his way along the so-called 'Path of Blood', those seventeen miles of dangerous and rocky road which slope from Jerusalem to Jericho. (To this day they are still dangerous.) Suddenly the robbers swoop, beat up their man, strip him of his valuables, and vanish as quickly as they came. A little later, along come, one after the other, two pillars of the Jewish church, a priest and a levite (one of the minor clergy). They cannot help seeing the robbers' victim, but they do not lift a finger to help. Were they just plain callous? Or did the remembrance of their sacred duties in the Temple prevent these clerics from defiling themselves by touching a corpse?[1] (No Jew could take part in a religious rite who had touched a corpse – see Num. 19.11.) Or were they afraid that the robbers might re-appear and knock them also on the head? We do not know. What we do know is that, human nature being what it is, good reasons have a way of presenting themselves when we are faced with a distasteful duty. So off go priest and levite on their famous wide detour: they 'passed by on the other side'.

Then along comes the true hero of the tale, and of all people he is a Samaritan – a half-breed heretic, a man (it has been said) with a half bible and mixed blood. One look at the victim is enough to move his pity. Dismounting, he applies his first-aid, wine and oil to disinfect the wounds and bandages to bind them up. Then, hoisting the man 'on his own beast' (Did he have another to carry his packs?), off he goes on to the nearest hostelry to care for him that night. Next morning, producing what, by our money values, would be something like 'two fivers' he said to the landlord, 'Look after him, and if you spend any more I will repay you on my way back'. (Note how lavish is the Samaritan's solicitude. This is Jesus' way of saying that it is the nature of true love to be extravagant.)

The story over, Jesus asks the final question, 'Which of these three men, do you think, proved neighbour to the man who fell among the robbers?' The lawyer gives him the only possible

[1] If so, they must have supposed the unconscious man already dead.

answer, 'The one who showed him kindness'. 'Then,' said Jesus, 'go and do as he did.'

III No story of Jesus, except the Prodigal Son, has so left its mark on our thinking and language. The Good Samaritan is in the gallery of immortal figures in imaginative literature, along with Bunyan's Pilgrim, Hamlet, and Don Quixote. But have we not tended to sentimentalize it? For us it is the story of the man who did his good deed. But is its point really the virtue of doing a good deed? Is it not that one's neighbour may well be the man we least expect, the Samaritan of the story? 'How can I love my neighbour if I don't know who he is?' the lawyer had asked. Jesus answers 'Love knows no bounds of race. It only asks for opportunities of going into action.'

The tale is really timeless. You can put it across, say, in South African terms.[2] The scribe then becomes the Afrikaner lawyer trying to define the term 'neighbour'; the victim a South African coloured; the priest and levite two ministers of the Dutch Reformed Church. For the Samaritan substitute a wayfaring Bantu.

When you think of it this way, it ceases to be just the story of the man who did his good deed, and becomes a damning indictment of all racial and religious superiority. And to the question 'Who is my neighbour?' Jesus still says, 'Wrong question. The right question is, To whom can I be one?' But he does not stop there. To all of us who call ourselves Christians, he says, 'Go and do what the Samaritan did to all the unfortunates you meet on life's "Path of Blood" '. Equally he says it to all nations calling themselves Christian; and for them the robbers' victim stands for all the broken men and the refugees and the victims of 'man's inhumanity to man'.

One final word. In the early days of the church men like Origen equated the Good Samaritan with Christ himself. Today we are inclined to react and say, 'Ah but this is to allegorize the parable. This is not scientific exegesis.' But if it is not exegetically right, is it not evangelically true? Did not the teller of the tale himself become, by his cross, the Good Samaritan of us all when for our hurt he gave us healing and brought us life by his death? If this is true, are we not under the most solemn obligation to

[2] G. V. Jones, *op. cit.*, 115.

honour and serve the hidden Christ who meets us in all his poor and hungry and unfortunate brothers?

Dives and Lazarus (*Luke 16.19-31*)

When the young Albert Schweitzer contrasted the wealth of Europe with the woes and misery of Africa, he concluded that the parable of Dives and Lazarus was 'spoken directly to us'. 'We,' he said, 'are Dives. Out there in Africa lies wretched Lazarus. And just as Dives sinned against Lazarus because, for want of heart, he never put himself in his place and let his conscience tell him what he ought to do, so we sin against the poor at our gate.'[3] So Schweitzer went off to Africa.

How do you read Jesus' famous story? Some have supposed that in it he was giving us a preview of the next world. Others have thought he was answering the question, Is there another chance in the next life for those who have failed in this one? Both views are mistaken. All the story tells us about the afterlife is that there *is* one and that our conduct here affects our destiny there. As for the background scenery – Abraham's bosom, the angels, paradise and hell, and so on – Jesus has simply drawn them from the current ideas of the time to serve as drapery for the truth he has to teach.

Consider the story again. What we have is really a little drama in two acts with an important epilogue appended.

In Act I (vv. 19-21) the scene is the visible world. Here is Dives decked out in 'purple and fine linen' (shall we say, in his Savile Row suitings) and 'faring sumptuously every day' (shall we say, drinking his gin and tonics and going the round of the races). Then, side by side, we are shown Lazarus in his rags at the rich man's gate, his body festering with ulcers which the roaming street dogs rasp with their tongues, while he himself only manages to keep alive by eating the bits of bread which the rich man's guests wipe their fingers on before throwing away. Dives in his luxury and finery, Lazarus in his rags and sores – this is the picture.

But when the curtain rises on Act II (vv. 22-6), the visible world has given place to the invisible one, and there has been

[3] *On the Edge of the Primeval Forest*, 1.

a dramatic change in the two men's fortunes. Before us now
appear heaven and hell on one small stage. But now Lazarus
reclines in Abraham's bosom at the heavenly banquet, while
Dives is in hell, racked by thirst and tormented in flame. Moreover, though Dives in life had never spared a glance for the
beggar at his gate, now he sees him – afar off and in felicity –
and would fain make him his friend. So he appeals to 'father
Abraham' for help from Lazarus, only to be told that it is too
late. 'Dives,' he is told, 'you got your good things in life, Lazarus
the ills. Now the fortunes are reversed.' Besides, 'between us and
you there is a great gulf fixed.' That is, God has made his judgment on your two lives and against that judgment there is no
appeal.

If the tale[4] ended there, its meaning would surely have been,
'The inhuman man is a lost soul. He goes into eternity without
a single friend'. But in verse 27 the conversation continues and
takes a different turn in what we have called the epilogue.

In this epilogue Dives asks Abraham to send Lazarus to warn
his five brothers lest a like fate befall them too. To understand
this, we must imagine the men who had heard Jesus' story
objecting, 'That is final all right, but is it fair? If Dives had
known what a roasting he was in for hereafter, how differently
he would have treated Lazarus on earth!' Or, more simply and
generally, if what we do, or fail to do, on earth matters so
much, we ought to be told so on evidence that no one can
doubt.

To this objection Jesus, speaking through the mouth of Abraham, replies: 'They have Moses and the prophets; let them listen
to them.' In other words, in the bible they already have a
sufficient guide on how they ought to live and they need no
more. But this does not satisfy Dives. 'Ah but,' he says, 'if only
someone could go back from the dead and warn them, this
would make them mend their ways.' Once again Jesus dismisses
the objection: 'If they do not listen to Moses and the prophets,
they will pay no heed even if someone should rise from the

---

[4] In vv. 19-26 Jesus may be using a popular tale about the reversal of
fortunes in the next life, in order to get through his hearers' (the Sadducees?) guard. They would hear the first part of the story approvingly
but be quite unprepared for the epilogue.

dead.' In plain prose, no reformed conduct in this life will be produced and promoted by more convincing evidence of the future life and future judgment.

We may now draw out the meaning and relevance of the parable.

First, whatever else it is, it is a lesson in humanity. We catch in it echoes of the same voice which said in the parable of the Last Judgment, 'Inasmuch as you did it to one of the least of my brethren ...' God meets us at our own door, and his question is, 'What have you done with Lazarus?' So Schweitzer understood it and responded to its challenge with a life spent in caring for his black brothers in the swamps of Lambarene. But if heroic self-sacrifice like Schweitzer's is possible only to a few, all Christians are called to do what they can to feed the hungry, clothe the naked, and help the helpless. For to perform such acts of love is, in Christ's phrase, to 'lay up treasures in heaven'; and that very fact can of itself make heaven real to the doers as it never can be to the hard-hearted and inhuman.

The other point comes in the epilogue.

The parable was probably spoken to the Sadducees[5] – the Sadducees who were rich and did not believe in an after-life. We know that Jesus engaged them in controversy, and it sounds as if they had asked from him some supernatural sign. They had sought to evade Jesus' challenge by saying that they might change their minds about the future life if only he would give them a supernatural sign in proof of it. Such a sign Jesus refuses to give. 'They will pay no heed even if someone should rise from the dead.'

Such a sign, he implies, would be quite valueless. Men are expected to respond to the revelation they have now, and not to postpone their response because they have not been given sufficient warrant of its supernatural origin. If they cannot respond to truth when they meet it, they are most unlikely to respond to some more unusual manifestation, if it could be provided.[6]

What Jesus says about this valueless sign is as true now as when he said it to the Sadducees. We have still among us

---

[5] T. W. Manson, *The Sayings of Jesus*, 296f.
[6] C. W. F. Smith, *The Jesus of the Parables*, 1948, 230-39.

many wealthy agnostics who refuse to believe in God or an
after-life and are deaf to the needs of suffering humanity. But
their refusal to believe and their failure to help are due, we may
suspect, not to a sincere 'rationalism' (like, say, T. H. Huxley's)
but to some other and less worthy cause. To all such Jesus says,
'If a man with the revelation of God's will before him in the
scriptures and Lazarus lying in misery on his doorstep, cannot
be humane, nothing – neither a visitant from another world nor
a revelation of the terrors of hell – will teach him otherwise.'

In short, to the inhuman man the next world will never be
more than a subject for unanswered questions; but 'for those who
live in a love like Christ's, it will be what it was for him –
another part of his Father's house, and as real as that which we
can see'.[7]

The Last Judgment (Matt. 25.31-46)

Of all Christ's parables this picture, or vignette, of the Last
Judgment is perhaps the most sombre and haunting. Doomsday
and eternal separation are its burden; and it tells of the hidden –
the disconcerting – Christ who comes to us, incognito, in his
poor and needy brothers.

I The parable is about the last thing modern man wants to
hear about – The Last Judgment. We live in a 'permissive age'
which has largely lost its sense of the reality of God, and men
would fain forget that they are finally accountable to the
Almighty for what they do in this life – or fail to do. Moral
distinctions have become blurred; sins now appear as amiable
weaknesses; and we tend to shuffle out of personal responsibility
for our misdeeds, pleading 'something came over me' and asking
the psychologist to explain what the 'something' was. Add to
this the contagious materialism of the age whose philosophy is
the old Epicurean one of 'Let us eat, drink and be merry, for
tomorrow we die'; and it is no wonder that many a modern
man rejects the Last Judgment as an exploded myth.

Yet if you believe in a living and righteous God, holding not
only that we are responsible for what we do but also that death

---

[7] J. Denney, *The Way Everlasting*, 176.

does not settle all scores, you cannot burke the issue or evade the problem. Stopford Brooke has posed it unforgettably:

> Three men went out one summer night,
> No care had they or aim,
> And dined and drank, 'Ere we go home,
> We'll have', they said, 'a game'.
>
> Three girls began that summer night
> A life of endless shame,
> And went through drink, disease and death
> As swift as racing flame.
>
> Lawless and homeless, foul they died,
> Rich, loved and praised the men,
> But when they all shall meet with God
> And justice speaks, what then?

Moreover, even a casual reading of the New Testament shows that Christ and the apostles believed in such a Judgment, declaring that even now men can, by what they do, or fail to do, help to judge themselves.

No doubt our forefathers to whom 'the great white throne' was no grand perhaps but a solemnizing certainty, sometimes painted the Judgment in colours no longer credible to those who have seen the love of God to sinners revealed in Christ. Yet no creed can be called truly Christian which does not affirm that we are finally accountable to our Maker.

II   And so to Christ's parable.

'When the Son of Man comes in his glory,' it begins, 'he will sit in state on his throne, with all the nations gathered before him.' Here the first question is, Who is the Judge? The answer is that 'the Son of Man', who later appears in the parable as 'the King', can only be Jesus himself. We cannot miss the tremendous claim he is making. The Carpenter of Nazareth declares that he will be the ultimate arbiter of man's destiny.

The second question is, Who are those being judged? 'All the nations' here must mean 'all the Gentiles'. We may see, then, in the parable Jesus' answer to the question, possibly asked by a disciple, 'By what criterion will those be judged who have never known you?' The answer of Jesus is, 'The heathen have met me in my brethren, for all the needy are my brothers. Therefore on the great Day, they will be judged by the compassion they have shown to the poor and afflicted in whom they have met me incognito; and if they have fulfilled the royal law of love, they will share in my Father's eternal kingdom.'

When Jesus says, 'Inasmuch as you have done it to me or the least of my brethren', by 'his brethren' he means not his disciples but all the wretched, forsaken and unfriended children of God. Such is Christ's solidarity with them that to show love to them is to show love to himself, and to refuse love to them is to refuse love to him. So the justification of those who have not known Christ will be a justification not by faith but by love. And if there is condemnation, by the same token it will be for lack of love to men and women in their miseries.

The parable has been called 'the story of the great surprises'; on the one hand, the unfeigned surprise of the 'blessed ones' who had, so to speak, stumbled into paradise, all unaware that in helping the needy they had been confronting Christ himself; and, on the other hand, the pained surprise of the condemned who would (they implied) have acted so very differently if only they had known that these poor, unfriended folk were in fact Christ's brothers.

III If the parable was originally Christ's answer to a question about the judgment of the heathen, it speaks its truth no less powerfully to Christians today. Through it Jesus still says, 'The grievous sins are those of inhumanity, and inhumanity is a sin which may invade any human heart'. And if the parable makes one thing clear, it is that he who holds in his hands the destiny of men cares utterly for the hungry, the sad, the naked, the stranger and the prisoner. As 'Jesus Christ is the same yesterday, today and for ever' (Heb. 13.8), these still remain the care and concern of him with whom we also will one day come face to face.

Thus our Lord's vignette of judgment, escaping out of the first century, asks us what we are doing now as Christians to care for the sick in body and mind, for all the derelicts and 'drop-out' of our society and our world. 'The church is her true self,' said Dietrich Bonhoeffer, 'only when she exists for others,' that is, when she becomes 'the caring church'. If this is true, the parable is a challenge to Christian action, a summons to us to become Christ's 'soldiers of pity' to the sore-stricken and unfortunate folk who meet us on life's road. We, too, it says, will be called to account for all we have done, or failed to do, for the least of Christ's brothers in whom he himself hiddenly confronts us.

If the tale of the Good Samaritan calls to Christian involvement with all the wounded ones we encounter on life's 'Path of Blood', even more does this one by setting the truth against the backdrop of the Last Judgment.

In one of his poems W. B. Yeats says:

> When we come at the end of time
> To Peter sitting in state;

but, according to the gospel, the one 'sitting in state' will not be Peter but Peter's Lord. And to us who in life have professed to follow him, he will not merely say, 'Did you call me Lord, Lord?' but will go on to ask, 'Did you turn your fine professions into acts of love for the poor and afflicted people who crossed your path, and in whom you met me in disguise?'

The hidden Christ? The Christ who confronts us in other people, especially the needy and unfortunate? We can, we often do, so meet him unawares. Do you remember that famous passage in Turgenev? He tells how, once as he worshipped in a simple country church, with peasant folk all around him, a man came up and stood by his side who, he felt, must be the Christ. But – he had 'a face like all men's faces'. 'What sort of Christ is this?' he said to himself. 'Such an ordinary, ordinary man. It cannot be.' He strove to resist the impression that it was the Christ, but in the end he could not. And at last the truth came home to him. 'Only then I realized,' he said, 'that just such a face – a face like all men's faces – is the face of Christ.'

None has better summed up the meaning of the parable than Henry Van Dyke:

> He that careth for a wounded brother
> Watcheth not alone:
> There are three in the darkness together,
> And the third is the Lord.

Happy he who thus finds Christ!

NOTE

On the authenticity of the parable see H. E. W. Turner's admirable article on it in *The Expository Times* for May, 1966. Cf. also my *Interpreting the Parables*, 118.

The Narrow Door (*Luke 13.23f*)

Someone asked Jesus, 'Sir, are only a few to be saved?' His answer was, 'Struggle to get in through the narrow door; for I tell you that many will try to enter and not be able'.

There is a breed of men we may call 'theological inquisitives'. They like to ask questions to which scripture gives no clear answer. Like the man who asked Luther, 'What was God doing before he made the world?' 'Looking round for a big stick,' replied Luther, 'to beat those who ask foolish questions.' Not all their questions have been quite so foolish as this. The one they have raised oftenest is the one put to Jesus somewhere on the road to Jerusalem: 'Sir, are only a few to be saved?' Jesus did not give a direct answer; but not a few down the centuries have been sure they knew the right answer. Burns's 'Holy Willie', in the eighteenth century was one of them:

> O Thou that in the heavens does dwell,
> Who, as it pleases best Thysel,
> Sends ane to heaven an' ten to hell
>   A' for Thy glory,
> And not for onie gude or ill
>   They've done afore Thee.

To such an answer the first Christian reaction must be, 'This cannot be the God and Father of our Lord Jesus Christ'. But Holy Willie might have retorted on us by quoting scripture. Did not Jesus say, 'Many are called, but few are chosen' (Matt. 22.14)? And again, 'Narrow is the gate and strait the way that leads to life, and few are those who find it' (Matt. 7.14)?

How shall we answer him, and all like him?

To begin with, we may agree that Jesus never said salvation was an easy thing. He would have agreed with Browning:

> How very hard it is
> To be a Christian!

To this we will come back, but meanwhile, let us note that in Matt. 22.14 'many' has the sense of 'all'. Jesus is not speaking primarily of God's selection by predestination, as Holy Willie certainly was; but of the boundlessness of God's invitation. God invites *all* men into his kingdom. And if the words 'but few are chosen' seem to support Holy Willie, we may reply that Christ's words are better taken dialectically. That is to say, we have here a paradox that warns us that our calling and election can never be taken for granted because we stand continually under the grace and judgment of God. 'There's nane of us right in,' said the old Highlander who had 'decided for Christ' at seventeen, to Dr George Macleod. 'There's nane of us right in: there's aye a wee murmur aboot the hert.'

But – and this is the second part of our reply – have we any right to deduce from two isolated scripture texts a complete eschatology (i.e., account of the Last Things and men's final destiny) enabling us to fix the populations of hell and heaven (as Holy Willie did) on a ten to one ratio? If the matter were to be settled simply by quoting texts, we might retort that, according to Jesus, '*many* will come from east and west and sit at table with Abraham, Isaac and Jacob in the kingdom of heaven' (Matt. 8.11), and that Jesus himself said that the purpose of his dying was to 'give his life as a ransom for many' – for all (Mark 10.45).

Yet even this is not the end of the answer. When that inquisitive man on the road to Jerusalem asked Jesus, 'Are only a few to be saved?' Jesus answered, 'Struggle to get in through the narrow door, for I tell you that many will try to enter and not be able'.

Jesus compares the way of salvation to a door which God opens and man enters. Without God man's entry cannot be made. But once the door is thrown open, man has to make his way in. Nor is entrance easy: it is a case of struggling rather than of strolling in: and if some fail to enter, it is not because God is unable to let them in, but because they refuse to enter on the only terms on which entrance is possible.

The truth is that Jesus turned the question of theological curiosity into what we would now call an 'existential' challenge – a challenge in terms of personal action and decision. We have no key to the eternal destiny of others except that which we have to our own. 'Are only a few to be saved?' was the question put to Jesus. Jesus' answer was: 'Few enough to make you afraid you may not be there. See to your entry.'

Is not that still the right answer to such a question?

Select Bibliography

BROWN, L. E., *The Parables of the Gospels*, 1913.

BRUCE, A. B., *The Parabolic Teaching of Jesus Christ*, 1882.

CADOUX, A. T., *The Parables of Jesus*, 1930.

DODD, C. H., *The Parables of the Kingdom*, 1935.

FINDLAY, J. A., *Jesus and His Parables*, 1950.

HUNTER, A. M., *Interpreting the Parables*, 1960.

JEREMIAS, J., *The Parables of Jesus*[2], 1963.

JONES, G. V., *The Art and Truth of the Parables*, 1964.

LINNEMANN, E., *Parables of Jesus*, 1966.

MANSON, T. W., *The Sayings of Jesus*, 1949.

MARTIN, H., *The Parables of the Gospels and their Meaning for Today*, 1937.

MONTEFIORE, C. G., *The Synoptic Gospels*, 1909.

OESTERLEY, W. O. E., *The Gospel Parables*, 1936.

SMITH, B. T. D., *The Parables of the Synoptic Gospels*, 1937.

SMITH, C. W. F., *The Jesus of the Parables*, 1948.

THIELICKE, H., *The Waiting Father*, 1960.

Index of Parables

Apprenticed Son (*John 5.19f.*), 14, 23, 25
Asking Son (*Luke 11.11-13; Matt. 7.9-11*), 14

Barren Fig Tree (*Luke 13.6-9*), 12, 21
Benighted Traveller (*John 12.35f.*), 23
Burglar (*Luke 12.39f.; Matt. 24.43f.*), 102

Callous Judge (*Luke 18.2-8a*), 21, 74, 81f.
Costly Pearl (*Matt. 13.45f.*), 21, 23, 74, 77ff.

Defendant (*Luke 12.57-9; Matt. 5.25f.*), 12, 21, 89, 90ff.
Disobliging Neighbour (*Luke 11.5-8*), 21, 74, 80ff.
Dives and Lazarus (*Luke 16.19-31*), 12, 28, 108, 112ff.
Drag Net (*Matt. 13.47f.*), 20, 48

Farmer and his Man (*Luke 17.7-10*), 21, 74, 83f.
Friend at Midnight. *See* Disobliging Neighbour

Good Employer (*Matt. 20.1-15*), 18, 20, 52, 70ff.
Good Samaritan (*Luke 10.30-7*), 10, 11, 12, 25, 108ff., 118
Grain of Wheat (*John 12.24*), 20, 22, 23, 35, 49ff.
Great Supper (*Luke 14.15-24*), 11, 12, 20, 21, 24, 25, 89, 93ff.

Hidden Treasure (*Matt. 13.44*), 21, 23 74, 77ff.

Importunate Widow. *See* Callous Judge

Labourers in the Vineyard. *See* Good Employer
Last Judgment (*Matt. 25.31-46*), 25, 108, 114, 115ff.
Leaven (*Luke 13.20f.*), 13, 19, 35, 43ff.
Little Ewe Lamb (*II Sam. 12.1-14*), 10, 24, 108
Lost Coin (*Luke 15.8-10*), 12, 20, 52, 56ff.
Lost Sheep (*Luke 15.3-7*), 11, 12, 15, 20, 52, 56ff.

Man in Charge (*Luke 12.42-8*), 90
Marriage Feast (*Matt. 22.1-10*), 93
Money in Trust. *See* Talents
Mote and the Beam. *See* Splinter and the Plank.
Mustard Seed (*Mark 4.30-32; Luke 13.18f.*), 14, 19, 24, 35, 43ff.

Narrow Door (*Luke 13.23f.*), 108, 119ff.

Owner's Son. *See* Wicked Vinedressers

Pharisee and Publican (*Luke 18-9-14*), 11, 52, 63ff.
Playing Children (*Matt. 11.16; Luke 7.31f*), 14
Precious Pearl. *See* Costly Pearl
Prodigal Son. *See* Waiting Father

Rascally Factor. *See* Unjust Steward
Rich Fool (*Luke 12.16-21*), 11

Savourless Salt (*Mark 9.50*), 21
Seed Growing Secretly (*Mark 4.26-9*), 19, 35, 39ff.
Seine-net. *See* Drag Net
Sheep and Goats. *See* Last Judgment

Sower (*Mark 4.3-9*), 14, 20, 24, 28, 35ff.
Sleeping Householder (*Luke 12.39*), 90
Splinter and the Plank (*Luke 6.41f.;
   Matt. 7.3-5*), 13
Stronger Man (*Mark 3.27*), 25

Talents (*Matt. 25.14-30*), 12, 17, 21,
   89, 96ff.
Tares. *See* Weeds among the Wheat
Ten Bridesmaids (*Matt. 25.1-13*), 12,
   15, 21, 89, 101ff.
Tower Builder (*Luke 14.28-30*), 20, 23,
   74ff.
Treasure Trove. *See* Hidden Treasure
True Shepherd (*John 10.1-15*), 23, 25
Two Builders (*Luke 6.47-9; Matt.
   7.24-27*), 12, 21, 25, 74, 85ff.
Two Debtors (*Luke 7.36-50*), 10, 20,
   52ff.
Two Houses. *See* Two Builders

Unforgiving Debtor (*Matt. 18-23-35*),
   30, 52, 67ff.

Unjust Steward (*Luke 16.1-8*), 11, 14,
   17, 18, 21, 89, 99ff.
Unmerciful Servant. *See* Unforgiving
   Debtor

Waiting Father (*Luke 15.11-32*), 11,
   12, 16, 17, 20, 25, 28, 30, 52, 56, 59ff.
Waiting Servants (*Luke 12.35-81*), 21,
   90, 102
Warring King (*Luke 14.31f.*), 20, 23,
   74ff.
Way to Court. *See* Defendant
Weather Signs (*Luke 12.54-6*), 90
Wedding Guests (*Mark 2.19f.*), 24
Weeds among the Wheat (*Matt.
   13.24-30*), 46ff.
Wicked Vinedressers (*Mark 12.1-12*),
   10, 12, 18, 22, 24, 25, 89, 104ff.
Wise and Foolish Bridesmaids. *See*
   Ten Bridesmaids
Woman in Labour (*John 16.21*), 23

Index of Biblical References

Leviticus
19.13   70
19.18   109

Numbers
19.11   110

Deuteronomy
6.5   109

II Samuel
12.1-14   10, 24, 108

Psalms
51.1   65
106.5   83

Ecclesiastes
4.9   56

Isaiah
5.1-7   104
40.9f.   43
52.7f.,   43
55.10f.,   19, 35

Jeremiah
31.27   19, 35

Ezekiel
ch.17   24
17.22f.   45
31.6   45
36.9   19, 35

Daniel
4.10ff.   45
4.20f.   45

Hosea
2.23   19, 35

Zechariah
10.9   19, 35

Matthew
chs. 5-7   86
5.3   96
5.25f.   90ff.
5.45   39
5.48   73
ch.7   21
7.7   83
7.11   14
7.24-27   85ff.
8.11   120
11.17   14
11.28   75
13.24-30   46ff.
13.44f.   77
13.47-50   48
ch.18   30
18.12ff.   15
18.23-35   67ff.
19.30   73
20.1-15   70ff.
20.8   73
20.16   71, 73
21.31   55
22.14   119, 120
23.13   64
24.5   104
25.1   104
25.1-12   101ff.
25.13   104
25.14-26   96ff.
25.31-46   49, 115ff.

Mark
1.14f.   43
1.15   19
2.10   24
4.3-8   35ff.
4.10-12   13

4.26-29   39ff.
4.30-2   **43ff.**
10.31   73
10.45   50, 61, 120
12.1-9   104
12.1-12   10
13.32   103

Luke
4.23   11
ch.6   21
6.35f.   84
6.36   69
6.46   85
7.36-50   30, 52ff., 68
7.40-3   10
9.31   74
9.57   74
10.25-37   10, 108ff.
11.5-8   80ff.
12.32   37
12.35-9   90
12.49f.   50
12.57-9   90ff.
13.18-21   43ff.
13.19   24
13.23f.   119ff.
13.30   73
13.34   105
14.11   64
14.15-24   93ff.
14.28-33   74ff.
ch.15   12, 20, 25, 30
15.1f.   56
15.1-10   56ff.
15.11-32   59ff.
16.1-8   99ff.
16.10-13   18
16.19-21   112
16.19-26   113
16.19-31   112ff.
16.22-6   112f.

Luke—cont.		12.27	50	4.5	47
17.7-10	83f.	12.32	51	4.7-12	51
18.2-8a	8off.	14.6	63	15.3	61
18.6	101	14.8	55		
18.7	83	15.1	25	II Corinthians	
18.8b	80	16.33	85	5.21	84
18.9-14	63ff.				
18.14b.	64	Acts		Ephesians	
19.41-4	21	14.13	79	3.8	79
John		Romans		Colossians	
1.11	103	1.15	98	3.2	79
3.29	24	5.8	62		
5.19f.	14	8.38f.	88	Hebrews	
7.17	26	10.17	30	13.8	117
12.23	50	13.13f.	29		
12.24	49ff.			Revelation	
12.25	51	I Corinthians		2.10	77

Index of Names and Authors

Archimedes, 51
Arnold, Edwin, 13
Augustine, 16, 29, 47, 63, 73
Austin, J. L., 31

Barth, Karl, 79
Black, M., 14
Bonhoeffer, Dietrich, 51, 73, 75, 76, 117
Booth, William, 58, 72, 73
Bridges, Robert, 59
Brooke, Stopford, 116
Browning, Robert, 119
Bruce, A. B., 17, 83
Bultmann, Rudolf, 26, 27, 84
Bunyan, John, 87, 111
Burns, Robert, 48, 55, 119

Caird, G. B., 57, 90
Cairns, David, 27
Cairns, Principal David, 87
Calvin, John, 17
Carlyle, Thomas, 51, 86
Chalmers, Thomas, 84
Churchill, Winston, 9
Claudius, Matthias, 33
Crashaw, Richard, 66

Debussy, 59
Denney, James, 39, 53, 115
Dodd, C. H., 18, 23, 26, 96
Dürer, A., 82

Eliot, T. S., 62
Emerson, R. W., 51

Findlay, J. A., 101
Forsyth, P. T., 63, 76, 79, 82, 89, 92
Francis, St, 73
Fuchs, Ernst, 25, 27, 29, 31

Gamaliel, Rabbi, 78

Heidegger, Martin, 27
Herbert, George, 48
Hügel, F. von, 76
Hunter, A. M., 50, 66, 80, 93, 119
Huxley, T. H., 115

Inge, W. R., 10
Irenaeus, 16, 78

Jeremias, J., 15, 16, 18, 23, 24, 25, 26, 28, 39, 53, 59
Joad, C. E. M., 86
John the Seer, St, 58, 77
Jones, G. V., 17, 27, 62, 105, 111
Jülicher, A., 17, 18, 23, 24, 60, 61

Kierkegaard, S., 26, 66
King, Mrs Hamilton, 51

Leitch, J. W., 37
Lincoln, Abraham, 82
Linnemann, E., 29, 69, 70
Luther, Martin, 17, 56, 73, 119

Macleod, George, 120
Maldonatus, 17
Manson, T. W., 13, 26, 27, 54, 59, 77, 114
Marcion, 78
Masefield, John, 50, 59
Meredith, George, 66
Milton, John, 82, 96
Mitton, C. L., 70
Montefiore, C. G., 57
Moule, C. F. D., 13, 24, 39, 103
Muir, Edwin, 62

Niebuhr, Reinhold, 52

Oglethorpe, General, 67
Origen, 16, 111

Paul, St, 47, 61, 64, 73, 78, 79, 87, 98

Read, David, 98
Rembrandt, 59
Ruskin, John, 78

Schweitzer, Albert, 92, 112, 114
Scott, Walter, 68
Shaw, G. B., 94
Smith, C. W. F., 25, 114
Smith, R. Gregor, 26
Spurgeon, Charles, 64
Stephen, St, 51
Stevenson, R. L., 68
Swift, Jonathan, 105

Temple, William, 46, 47, 51, 58
Tennyson, Alfred, Lord, 28, 82
Tertullian, 16
Thielicke, H., 28, 59, 63
Thiselton, A. C., 31
Thomas Aquinas, 17
Thomson, W. M., 45
Toplady, T., 84
Turgenev, 118
Turner, H. E. W., 119

Van Dyke, Henry, 118

Wesley, John, 67, 72, 73
Wodehouse, P. G., 10, 53, 108

Yeats, W. B., 118

CPSIA information can be obtained
at www.ICGtesting.com
Printed in the USA
BVHW040956100220
571800BV00014B/28

4341241

DATE DUE

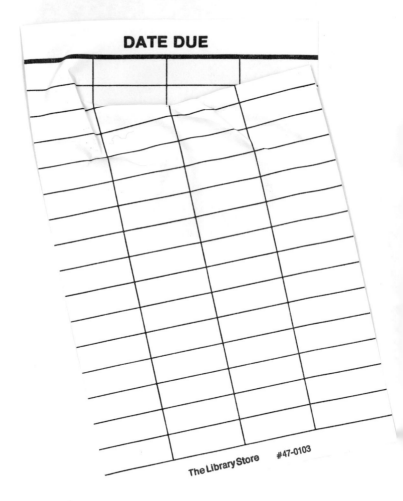

The Library Store   #47-0103